Praise for *Baby Out of W*

CO-PARENTING BASICS FROM PREGNANCY TO CUSTODY

I highly recommend Baby Out of Wedlock *to anyone who wants to learn the complicated dynamics of co-parenting while emphasizing the child's needs first.*
— **Kevin Falkenstein, Family Law Attorney and Partner,**
Moustakas Nelson LLC

My work focuses on what can eventually happen in a worst-case situation. Unmarried parents who read Baby Out of Wedlock *are taking a first step in the right direction.*
— **Ginger Gentile, Director & Producer of the documentary** *Erasing Family*
and one of Maria Shriver's Architects of Change

In my behavioral health practice, I often see the emotional toll that custody battles have on unmarried parents and their children. Baby Out of Wedlock *can make a difference in both parents' and their children's long-term mental health.*
— **Francesca Santacroce, Licensed Marriage and Family Therapist**
and Owner, Serenity Behavioral Health

When a client is knowledgeable about the basics of family law, it makes my job easier, and everyone benefits. Baby Out of Wedlock *is a great primer for anyone navigating the pregnancy-to-custody continuum.*
— **Jessica E. Smith, Family Law Attorney and Partner, JSDC Law Offices**

Pregnancy out of wedlock can be an incredibly scary experience. This book, with its emphasis on the importance of mental health, is a great guide. It helps readers know they are not alone.
— **Rachel Cohen, Licensed Mental Health Counselor**
and Clinical Supervisor, The Soho Center in New York City

Baby Out of Wedlock *provides answers to all the basic questions that inevitably challenge a co-parenting relationship. If both parents read this book, they can work together with less stress and anxiety while limiting the cost of lawyers.*
— **Andrew Keegan, Actor and Co-Parent**

My work is all about how people get through adversity, and Baby Out of Wedlock *has nailed its topic. Jim & Jessica Braz have written stories of who people need to be in order to navigate this experience. With their guidance, both parents and kids can live free of hostility, pain, and anguish.*
— **Bob Litwin, Performance Coach**
and Author of *Live the Best Story of Your Life*

Custody battles can spiral out of control if you let them. Baby Out of Wedlock *helps both parents realize that compromise is always the best way forward.*

— Michael Schwartz, CFP, AEP, CEO of Magnus Financial Group LLC,
and Divorced Father

I have been a licensed psychologist for over twenty-five years specializing in relationship and parenting issues, and I have known Jim and Jessica for over a decade. Their experience is real and their advice is practical. I highly recommend Baby Out of Wedlock *to anyone who finds themselves in this situation.*

— Lenore Perrott, MS, Psychologist

I highly recommend Baby Out of Wedlock *for anyone looking for honest, fair, and real-life experience during the stressful time from pregnancy to custody and beyond. It is an excellent resource as it places the child's best interest paramount while working toward the all-important co-parenting relationship.*

— Patricia A. Cummings, Licensed Certified Social Worker-Clinical,
Maryland Court Certified Parenting Coordinator

I've known Jim for over twenty years, and I remember when his daughter was born and how hard he had to struggle for parenting rights. His story is real, and his advice comes from experience.

— Lisa Benson, Vice President, IMG Models

Jessica made her share of mistakes in the early days, but since then she has clearly figured out how to make her co-parenting relationship successful. Read her book if you want to learn what works.

— Olena Zinshtein, Stepparent and Owner of Key Nutrition LLC

A great book that will clearly help anyone in a similar situation. The potential cost alone in navigating the process can be overwhelming, but this guide delivers sound advice and lessons learned. Well written and comprehensive.

— Patrick Donohue, US Army Pilot and Father

Baby
–Out of–
Wedlock

CO-PARENTING BASICS
FROM PREGNANCY TO CUSTODY

JIM & JESSICA BRAZ

softcover: 978-1-7368168-0-6
ebook: 978-1-7368168-1-3

Editor: Kim Bookless
Book Designer: Diana Russell Design
Publishing Strategist: Holly Brady
Cover photo courtesy of Shutterstock

The events described in this book are based on actual events, but the names and personal details of the people involved, including the authors, have been changed to protect their privacy and their children's emotional development. Some other minor details have been changed for illustration purposes.

Jim and Jessica Braz are not lawyers. While they have real-life experience in the issues discussed here, they do not give legal advice in this book. Furthermore, child custody laws, child support calculations, and family law, in general, vary from state to state. Be sure to consult an attorney in the appropriate state for your custody litigation.

Jim and Jessica Braz are not doctors. While they have real-life experience in the issues discussed here, they do not give medical advice in this book. Be sure to consult your doctor on your specific medical situation.

Jim and Jessica Braz are not licensed therapists, mediators, or counselors. While they have real-life experience in the issues discussed here, you should consult licensed professionals as needed.

The advice given in this book does not hold Jim and Jessica Braz legally liable for any adverse outcomes you may have from following their advice.

Jim.Jessica.Braz@BabyOutOfWedlock.com

Contents

1 | Why Read This Book?

According to research recently posted on the CDC website, *nearly 40%* of all births in the United States are to unmarried parents. That equals approximately 1,500,000 children born out of wedlock *every year*. Many of their 3,000,000 parents are worried, confused, and searching for answers. By comparison, there are only about 800,000 divorces in the United States each year.

If you are holding this book, then either you or someone you know has recently found out about an unexpected pregnancy. You are not married to the other parent-to-be, but you are weighing all the possibilities. You may have known the other person for years or barely more than one night. A hundred questions are going through your mind, and you have not slept well since you heard the news. In short, you are freaking out.

Purpose of This Book

The purpose of this book is to help the millions of new or soon-to-be mothers or fathers who are *not* in a traditional happy marriage. Ideally, you picked up this book the day after you heard the news, but more realistically, it's at least partway through the pregnancy or even past the birth. That's fine; this book will help you navigate nine months of pregnancy and get you through at least the first year of your child's life and then some.

If you are happily married or happily engaged, or even if you just know your partner is "the one," then this book *is not* for you. You will have challenges as all parents do, but this book does not address them. There are lots of other books out there for you.

This book *is* for anyone in a serious long-term relationship, a casual short-term relationship, or even just a one-night stand that resulted in a pregnancy. It could also help anyone who is surprised by pregnancy with someone they are about to divorce, especially if it is your first child together.

This book is *not* about endorsing any single parenting style, but it *is* about learning how to be a great co-parent by getting off to the right start during the pregnancy.

This book *is* about learning from our personal mistakes and learning to see your co-parent's point of view to help you make better decisions for your child.

This book *is* about learning your rights and responsibilities as unmarried co-parents.

This book is *not* a substitute for a good family lawyer. Instead, it is a supplement, a navigation tool, and a lot cheaper than asking your lawyer every little question that pops in your head.

This book *is* about protecting your parenting rights while also "doing what's right" for the child, who will be best served by *two* involved parents.

If you are under eighteen, then you have extra challenges ahead of you that this book does not address except to say you will need to seek help from loved ones.

This book is designed to give you the answers you are looking for efficiently and straightforwardly. We know you are not in the mood for long-winded lessons or clever anecdotes right now. You want straight-talk answers ASAP.

What Makes Us Experts?

Why us? It's true my wife, Jessica, and I are not experts. We don't have PhDs in family or childhood development. We are not lawyers or therapists. If you want that kind of academic advice, there are probably better books out there. However, if you want real-world information that gets results and *works*, this is the book for you.

My wife and I wrote this book because about ten years ago, before we were a couple, we both lived through the same situation you are going through now. I had a daughter, and Jessica had a son, with other people we did not want to marry. We made a lot of mistakes back then. We learned from those mistakes, and we want to share what we learned with you.

We remember all the questions we had back then and how hard it was to get straight answers. Again, this book is not a substitute for a good family lawyer. You will definitely need a lawyer in this process, but you don't need to pay them an arm and a leg if you read this book carefully.

We hope this book will save you money by answering many of the "dumb" questions running through your mind right now, thereby keeping your lawyer's billable hours to a minimum. The book's price and the time it takes you to read it is nothing compared to the tens (maybe hundreds?) of thousands of dollars you can spend defending your parental rights. Jessica and I paid ungodly sums on legal bills (you'll need to read on to find out how much exactly) just to establish standard legal custody and visitation rights with our babies out of wedlock, and our two cases never even went to trial.

If you take the advice in this book seriously, you shouldn't need to spend much on lawyers. If both parents read this book, the results will be even better, and your child will benefit from two cooperative and civil co-parents who understand and respect each other's roles.

Jim's Story

I don't want to get too personal with my story's details, but I want to give you enough background information to know the experience I'm offering you is legitimate. Your story will undoubtedly be different, but I guarantee you will face many of the same challenges I did.

It was Christmas week about twelve years ago when I reunited with an old flame; let's call her Mary to protect her identity. We had never slept together before this reunion night. It was consensual. We were both about thirty years old. I was raised in the suburbs of Philadelphia and was mildly successful at a bank in Manhattan. Mary was an executive assistant who had lived in Manhattan for a couple of years when we had dated a while back. At the time of our reunion, she was living in Arizona, and she loved it there. She grew up outside of Washington, DC, and her family was still there.

A couple of years before the fateful night she became pregnant, Mary and I had a relationship that lasted a few months. So we were not strangers, but we were not dating when she got pregnant. It was just one of those nights where one thing led to another and, well, you know. I had always practiced very safe sex my entire life, but I let my guard down this particular night. For her part, Mary had been practicing celibacy for a while at the time, waiting for marriage, but on this night, well, I guess she let her guard down too.

Some readers may assume that Mary tried to trap me by getting pregnant on purpose. I don't think that's what happened for several reasons, one of them being that she was a very religious person. She belonged to a specific religion that didn't look kindly on premarital sex. For her, having a baby out of wedlock would have caused more than the typical amount of social stigma.

She may have just felt she was getting older, and it was time to start taking some chances. She might have assumed if it was God's will to give her a child, then we would just get married. Maybe that's what she thought, maybe not. But the point is, I don't think she tried to "trap" me in any way.

I'll tell more of my story with Mary as we move through the issues, but for now, you should also know that Mary and I were both never married to anyone before the pregnancy, and we had no other kids before our daughter, Kelly, was born.

Perhaps the most significant thing to know about me for this book is that I am a type A person. A planner. Punctual. A rational decision-maker. "Anal," Mary would say. I'm a by-the-book type of guy. I like to travel by train because they are efficient and reliable (this becomes important later in my story). Mary is the opposite; she prefers flexibility and likes last-minute decisions. She doesn't adhere well to schedules. She is an emotional decision-maker. She prefers to travel by car because they are more flexible and give her a feeling of control, even though she knows that, statistically, highways are more dangerous than trains. Mary is type B all the way. Unfortunately, we were both opinionated beyond belief, and neither of us was a pushover.

In short, our personalities were a recipe for disaster, and we both knew it and decided early on not to get married. We were long-distance during the pregnancy, and every communication between us seemed to escalate into an argument. I was to blame for at least half those arguments for sure. The result was that by the time her due date rolled around, Mary and I were not on speaking terms, and I was starting to wonder if she had given birth without telling me and had possibly even gone into hiding with our child. It was not a good situation, but it was one you should be able to avoid if you read this book.

Jessica's Story

Jessica has a story that is similar but different from mine. She, too, was around thirty years old when she got pregnant unexpectedly. But Jess was dating her guy at the time, and for a while, they thought they might stay together and perhaps get married.

We'll call him Bill, and as with Mary, we are changing some of the unimportant background details to protect his identity. However, Jessica and I want to say now, in the beginning, that although we had our differences with Bill and Mary, this book is not meant to trash-talk them in any way. They are great parents to our children, and we have enormous respect for both of them. Any mention of our experiences with Bill and Mary in the book are meant only to illustrate to the reader some examples of what can go wrong if you don't learn from our mistakes. We will try to be fair and point out our faults as well as theirs.

Anyway, Jessica and Bill were dating for a year or two when she got pregnant by total surprise. Doctors had told Jess when she was younger that she would have trouble conceiving due to an irregularly shaped uterus, so perhaps she was less careful about birth control than she could have been.

Jessica was a registered nurse at Pennsylvania Hospital, and Bill was a hotel manager, where they both lived in Philadelphia. Bill was a few years older than Jess. Once they got over the pregnancy shock, they started to plan a life together with a baby coming.

As with Mary and me, the details don't matter too much here, but suffice it to say they found themselves incompatible as a couple a few months into the pregnancy. By the time her son, Adam, was born—six months before my daughter—Jessica and Bill were not on speaking terms either.

For background, both Bill and Jessica's parents were divorced. Jess and I both grew up in the suburbs of Philadelphia, and Bill grew up in Pittsburgh. Both Jess and Bill had good people in their lives, but I think it's fair to say both of them probably had a more challenging childhood than Mary and I did.

Your Story

Now that you have our background, you may be thinking, *Jim and Jessica are nothing like me because*…Indeed, our stories are undoubtedly different from yours in one way or another. These days, we are much more aware of how large a role race and socioeconomic backgrounds can play in people's lives. You may have inferred from the previous pages that all four of us never had to deal with racial discrimination, poverty, or abusive family relationships in our lives. If you are thinking that our circumstances are not nearly as challenging as yours, you might be partially right, but that doesn't mean there is nothing to learn from our experiences when it comes to having a baby born out of wedlock.

For example, one of Jessica's biggest problems was that Bill got poor legal advice from an attorney friend who did not practice family law. This led to a lot of simple misunderstandings that could easily have been avoided. Make sure you choose a lawyer specializing in *family law*; a friend working pro bono will cause more harm than good if he doesn't practice family law.

This book is filled with little bits of advice like that, and most of it applies to anyone having a baby out of wedlock, regardless of race or socioeconomic background. Although your circumstances, history, and relationship with your co-parent are unique, most of what we discuss over the rest of the book will still apply to your story. If there are parts that don't, well, we hope you will be able to modify the information for your particular situation. If not, contact us on our website (BabyOutOf-Wedlock.com), and we might be able to point you to someone who can help.

Changing Your Story

Speaking of stories, it may help readers cope with this difficult situation if they realize the power they have to change their story. For years, we have worked with a motivational coach, Bob Litwin (BobLitwin.com), who wrote *Live the Best Story of Your Life*. His book is mostly about finding success in sports and business, but it applies to any challenge, including what you are going through now.

If you constantly tell yourself this pregnancy is a disaster, a nightmare, or someone else's fault, then you will stay stuck in the mental abyss you may feel you are in right now. On the other hand, if you start telling yourself another story, a positive story, then your reality will start to change for the better immediately.

When we say, "Tell yourself a positive story," we mean literally, *tell yourself* a positive story. Instead of waking up in the morning and feeling like a victim or unlucky or some other form of despair, try repeating a different line. Even say it out loud. It may seem like just words at first, but eventually, your brain will start to think differently.

For example, the negative story is that this pregnancy threw your life into a tailspin. The positive story is that this baby will give your life new meaning and purpose.

The old story is that you don't have enough money to legally defend your parenting rights, certainly not tens of thousands of dollars, so why bother even trying? The new story is that you are learning which issues attorneys can help with and which they cannot, and how you can get this done right without spending a fortune on legal bills. You just need to figure out what is worth fighting over and what is not.

The pessimistic story is that your co-parent is impossible to deal with and you are never going to see eye to eye. The optimistic story is that you will get along better with your co-parent once you learn how their brain works and get a few uncertainties answered in due time.

Again, this book is packed with advice that can help you change your baby-out-of-wedlock story. Will you use it? Will you actually start telling yourself a different story today? If you have to read this book twice for it to sink in, will you read it twice? Will you ask your co-parent to read it too? If you need to look for other coaches, therapists, or mental health professionals, will you also take that step? Or will you let yourself fall deeper into the abyss?

Enough preaching. Let's get started with what you need to know to survive the next few years. If your child is already born, you may be tempted to jump ahead to chapter 6, but we recommend you at least skim chapters 2 through 5 because there is some information in them that still applies to you.

2 | Surprise, I'm Pregnant

"I'm pregnant" are perhaps two of the most shocking words a person can utter. It's a negative surprise for some, and for others, it's a positive one, but no matter what, you are likely to remember for your entire life where you were and how you felt when you first said or heard those two words.

Women usually discover the news on their own from a pregnancy test, or perhaps from a doctor, but the shock can be just as great. Jessica took a pregnancy test, and then four more to be sure, when her period was late by a few days. If you are a woman reading this book, it's probably not the right time in your life to be pregnant, or maybe you are not with the man you wanted to have children with, and the pregnancy news probably felt surreal.

I remember I was at dinner with family on a Friday night in Manhattan when I got Mary's call. We had not been getting along very well since our "reunion" night, and I had a strange feeling when I saw her name ringing on my mobile phone that there was only one reason she would be calling me right now.

My gut was right. I took the call outside the restaurant. She said in a tearful voice, "Jim, I'm pregnant. You're the father. I expect you to be responsible, and I hope you want to be involved." I replied that I did want to be involved, and I definitely would be responsible, and I would call her back as soon as I came out of shock.

You no doubt have a similar story, and by now, it is sometime in the past, so we don't want to waste too much time on this chapter aside from one crucial point to make about paternity tests before we move on to more significant issues.

Paternity Tests

If you are the woman in the story, you may or may not be sure who the father is. Mary was sure it was me because she hadn't slept with anyone else, just as Jess knew it was Bill. Women with multiple partners cannot be sure who the father is without a test, and they should admit to themselves and their partners if there is uncertainty.

If you are the man in the story, your first reaction to the "I'm pregnant" news might be, "Are you sure I'm the father?" This is a fair question, but you want to be careful how you ask it.

Men need to keep in mind that the woman is not telling you this news unless she is pretty damn sure you are the father, and the last thing she wants to hear at this most stressful moment is you don't believe her or you think she must have slept around with multiple people recently. That kind of response is nothing but a punch in the gut.

However, women should remember that while they may be 100% certain who the father is, the man does not have that same degree of certainty because he does not know for sure who else you have been with besides him. Jess was insulted at first when Bill asked for a paternity test three months after

Adam was born. Her lawyer was right to explain that Bill just wanted to be 100% sure, as sure as Jess was.

Raising a child is a lifetime commitment. Both parents deserve to be 100% certain who the father of the child is. Certainty is a good thing for all parties involved, including the child. Fortunately, it is easy enough to test for paternity with a cheek swab once the child is born. Your lawyer should insist on this test, and the courts will always order the test if either party requests it. In many jurisdictions, a paternity test is standard operating procedure.

Testing for parentage before birth requires extracting amniotic fluid from the mother's belly. It is not a riskless process, and while it may be appropriate in some extreme circumstances, it is probably not the right move for most readers. We believe the father cannot force the mother to take a pre-birth paternity test against her will. Most of you can wait until the child is born to test for paternity.

So guys, try your best not to dispute her when you hear the words, "I'm pregnant, and you are the father." And ladies, try not to be defensive if he asks, "Are you sure it's mine?" Neither parent should spend their time and energy arguing about a paternity test. A test will happen in due time if either of you wants it to happen. Both of our babies born out of wedlock had paternity tests performed even though none of us were disputing paternity.

The best thing a man can do when he learns about the pregnancy is to be supportive and take responsibility for his actions. If you slept with her, then there is at least a chance you are the father. Put yourselves in her shoes; she is probably more worried and scared than you are. Even if the child turns out not to be yours, for the time being, assume it is so you can move forward without needlessly upsetting the mother-to-be.

3 | First Things First

You certainly don't need to decide the weighty issues in this chapter before reading the rest of this book, but you will need to resolve them soon. These may be some of the most difficult choices you make in your entire life—or the easiest, depending on your perspective. Let's make sure you are thinking about the issues clearly and understand who has the ultimate decision-making power.

Abortion?

The first question mothers face is whether to keep the pregnancy or pursue an abortion. For some mothers like Mary and Jess, this was not even a question. They knew from day one that they were going to keep their babies, no matter how difficult it would be or what Bill and I had to say about it. Abortion was not an option for them, partly for religious reasons, but also because they were entering their thirties and knew they might not have another chance at motherhood. I am pro-life in principle, so I agreed with Mary's decision, but it is a deeply personal decision that each *mother* has to make for herself.

We wrote "each mother" and not "each parent" because abortion is the mother's decision to make. If the mother wants to keep the baby and the father wants an abortion, Mom wins. If the father wants to keep the baby and the mother doesn't, well, Mom wins again. It's her body, and although you occasionally hear of a father asking the courts to force a woman to carry his baby to term, in practice, it's pretty much impossible to stop a woman who is determined to end her pregnancy.

The decision to abort will affect you for the rest of your life. You should get counseling before you decide, not just from a professional counselor but also from family and friends you respect. We believe the wisdom that comes with age is best for this sort of decision, so give more weight to advice from older folks who have the benefit of hindsight.

Hindsight is an amazing thing. I was scared to death when I found out Mary was pregnant. I'm sure Bill was, too, when he learned about Jessica's pregnancy. If Mary had said to me, "I'm going to get an abortion," I would have been distraught but probably felt some relief, too, if I'm honest about it. However, with the benefit of just a little hindsight, I can definitively say that my daughter, Kelly, was the best thing that ever happened to me. I am grateful Mary had the courage to choose life.

Jess and I think it's helpful for parents to consider the abortion question by transplanting themselves into old age many decades from now. Ask yourself which is more likely: Will you someday look back and regret raising a child, or is it more likely you will look back and regret having an abortion?

Regardless of how you answer that question, the point of this section is to make sure the father understands that abortion is ultimately the mother's decision. He should be honest with her so she can make the best decision possible.

If either parent plans to disappear and not be in the child's life, then at least have the decency to say so now rather than later. Just understand that you will likely be on the hook for child support if the other parent asks the courts for it, even if you don't want to be involved in raising the child. We will discuss child support in chapter 7.

Abortion laws vary from state to state, and the federal laws (Roe v. Wade) could change someday, too, so we cannot advise you on how or where to get an abortion if that is what you choose to do. But we recommend you finish reading this book before choosing abortion because you may change your mind when you realize being an unmarried co-parent is not as terrible as you may think.

Adoption?

If you decide to keep the pregnancy, the next question is whether you will raise the child yourself or give him up for adoption. The adoption decision can be even more difficult if you are especially young parents or if the pregnancy resulted from rape or other extreme circumstances. This book cannot address every situation or age bracket, but we certainly acknowledge that having our children at age thirty was less challenging than if we had been only twenty.

I wrote in the previous section that I was grateful Mary had the courage to choose life. Giving your child up for adoption also requires courage if you know you are not capable of raising a child for whatever reason. Carrying your child to term for nine months only to say goodbye after birth in some ways takes more courage than keeping the child in what you know is a hostile environment. Every situation is different, and the decision can torment you for life.

If you are a pregnant teenager, you have more challenges than older, more established individuals like Jess and I had to deal with. Raising the child will require extra help from loved ones besides the father, who probably is also very young. Most of the advice in this book still applies to you, but if you don't have the benefit of family and a support network around you to lean on, adoption *might* be the best choice for you. On the other hand, while having a child at a young age means you will be giving up some freedom in your twenties, you will gain freedom in your forties. Think long-term and realize you are not the first person to do this. Everything can work out fine if you think things through.

Adoption, like abortion, is one of the most difficult decisions a person can make. There are professionals out there who can help you work through these issues, and you should seek them out before you make your decision. It may be tempting to look for some sort of middle ground, like an arrangement where someone adopts your child but you visit occasionally. This is known as an "open adoption," and there will be a legal document that dictates your level of involvement with your child if you go this route. It may be the right choice for some people.

Again, this might be easy for us to say, given we didn't have any challenges like poverty, rape, or abuse to deal with, but our advice is to try to avoid the "middle ground" path. There is no simple middle ground when it comes to parenthood, and you may be doing the child a disservice if he spends his life comparing you to his legal guardian.

We think the same analysis applies to adoption as it does to abortion. Try to think about what you might regret more when you are old and gray—raising your child or giving him up for adoption.

Both parents should know, if the mother wants to give the child up for adoption, the biological father will probably have the right of first refusal. And it might be obvious, but a father cannot force a mother to give her child up for adoption.

Single Parent, Co-Parent, or Married Parents?

If you have decided to keep the pregnancy and raise your child rather than give him up for adoption, then the next question is what your relationship with the other parent will be like. You can take essentially three paths: single parent (child knows only one of you), co-parent (child knows both of you, but you're not a couple), or married parents.

If you love the other parent and want to spend your lives together, then, by all means, get married now, during the pregnancy. We can think of more than a few people who got married during an unexpected pregnancy and lived happily ever after for decades to come. In the old days, this was quite common. You can keep reading this book, but a lot of it won't apply to you once you're married.

On the other extreme, you might become a truly single parent, but that is not ideal for the child, and it's usually not something you can choose on your own. What we mean is, the other parent has to decide to be absent; you cannot choose to keep them away, nor can you make them stay if they don't want to. If one parent wants nothing to do with their child, you cannot force them to spend time parenting. However, they will always be on the hook for financial support unless they sign away their parental rights to a foster or stepparent.

If your child's other parent dies or runs away, never to be heard from again, then you will be a single parent (for now anyway). If the father is the Antichrist himself who raped the mother, perhaps it's possible to get the courts to keep him away from the child, but that would be pretty extraordinary. Even parents with substance abuse problems get some limited or supervised access to their children.

Assuming the other parent wants to be involved, or even if they disappear and then come back after an absence, it is a good bet the courts will not allow you to deny them access to their biological child. Therefore, being a single parent is not something most people can choose; it is a situation some people are left with.

Children benefit from two parents' dual perspectives. Traditionally, this means a mother and father, but same-sex couples can provide the same range of perspectives (however, it's unlikely a same-sex couple would have an unplanned pregnancy). Two parental points of view are usually better than one, even if you don't think highly of the other parent. If you are a single parent, well, you don't have much reason to keep reading this book past chapter 5.

If you are not a single parent, make sure to always keep in mind that two parents are better than one as you discuss your child during the pregnancy and after the birth. You will frequently disagree with your co-parent, but if you try to remember that the child benefits from two points of view, even when they are at odds, it will help foster a healthy relationship between the three of you.

Should You Get Married Now? Later? Ever?

Assuming you are not going to be a single parent, then the likely question before you now is whether or not you will marry this person. This is where the rubber meets the road for most people reading this book. Many parents-to-be are just not sure whether they should get married, and the pressure of the pregnancy makes them feel they must decide immediately. We disagree.

Mary and I were long-distance during her pregnancy, and at first, I thought maybe it was my duty to get married right away and make it work. However, I realized a "shotgun wedding" would just create a very high probability of divorce in a number of years, probably when the child was at a vulnerable age. I calculated that by getting married right away, I would be putting the odds in favor of a worse-case outcome (divorce) for my child.

I was open to the possibility of falling in love with Mary and getting married down the road, but I wanted it to happen naturally. I wanted to get married because of love and desire to be together, rather than because of some self-imposed timeline. I knew we had butted heads a lot when we dated years ago, and I figured it was foolish to think we would suddenly get along better because we shared a child.

I also realized that while divorce can tear a young child apart, if Mary and I were cooperative co-parents from the beginning, then our child would never know anything else. She may wonder why Mom and Dad were not under one roof someday, but she would never have to go through a painful separation.

It suddenly became clear that forcing marriage during pregnancy was the wrong choice for Mary and me. If you asked Mary, I'm sure she would agree that we made the right choice not to get married, even though at first she may have felt some stigma of being a single mother. If she ever had any marriage thoughts, I think they quickly faded after a few months of bickering during the pregnancy.

Jessica had a slightly different situation in that she was happily dating and maybe even in love when she got pregnant from Bill. But just a few months of apartment hunting and baby planning together during the pregnancy made them realize they were incompatible for marriage. One argument led to another during that stressful time. It's hard enough to move in or to raise a child together, but doing both at the same time is downright near impossible unless you are already totally committed to each other for life.

We have a friend who just learned she was pregnant, unexpectedly, this past year. She was in a committed relationship and in love at the time it happened. She is nearly forty, so she was getting very nervous about her biological timeline, knowing it would be harder to have kids each year. Her parents were old-fashioned and wanted her to be married before the baby came.

Our friend and her guy moved in together during her pregnancy. By the time their baby arrived, they were still unsure about marriage, yet they were attached at the hip due to a shared apartment lease. If they get married, they might always wonder whether it's what they truly wanted or they just took the path of least resistance. Do these marriages have a high divorce rate?

If you are in love but not sure yet about marriage or living together, then we strongly suggest you take it one step at a time. First, get your baby born safely. Support each other during pregnancy. Be there for each other and the child when he is born. If you fall in love and find you work well as a team, then after the birth, and after you've proved to each other where your priorities are, get engaged and make plans to move in together.

On the other hand, if the two of you find you are not a good match and Cupid does not shoot you with the love arrow, then you will have a solid foundation to become happy, healthy, supportive *co-parents*. You won't have any regrets or divorce baggage. And your child will never know anything different than "Mom and Dad both take great care of me and work as a team even though they don't live together."

The remainder of this book assumes you are not getting married (in the near term) and you are not doing it alone as a single parent. You might get married down the road, but for now, you are *co-parents*, and you will need to learn to work together.

4 | Play Nice

You have probably heard that your needs will take a back seat to your child's once you become a parent. This is common knowledge; we all know parents sacrifice a lot for their children.

But chances are good, especially if this will be your first child, that you may not yet fully understand what this means even if the baby has already arrived. You may still be thinking of parenthood as a minor challenge or an inconvenience, or a problem that is solvable with a few quick strokes. You may be telling yourself that not much in your life will change. You would be wrong.

This chapter may seem like a lot of "fluff" because it doesn't answer any cold, hard questions such as those about child support calculations. But Jess and I can say with experience that the advice below could be the most critical thing you get out of this entire book. Take it seriously, and your relationship and your stress levels will stay manageable. Ignore this advice, and you will find yourself in the same nightmares Jess and I were in during our respective situations.

Freaking Out

First, take a deep breath and just admit you are freaking the hell out. You've heard stories and seen movies, but you never thought *you* would be having a baby *like this*. You pictured your life differently. Perhaps you wanted to be married for at least two years before you had kids. Maybe your parents would never approve of having a child out of wedlock. Perhaps your church is causing you anxiety. Other readers may be in the middle of school or a big career move, and pregnancy just doesn't fit in with that schedule. Perhaps you were just about to relocate across the country for whatever reason, but now you have to consider someone else's geography.

Like Mike Tyson famously said, "Everyone has a plan until they get punched in the face." That's just life. You are not cursed. You are not a fool. Things happen. Your life will go on, that is for sure. Once you stop freaking out, you may realize this could be one of the best things that ever happened to you.

When I found out Mary was pregnant, I went into a state of shock at first. I don't recommend this, but I got pretty drunk that first night. And the next. And many other nights during the pregnancy when I was alone wondering how *it* would all work out. My stress and anxiety levels were through the roof, just as yours probably are right now. It must have been twice as hard for Mary, who couldn't numb her emotions with booze or anything else for fear of harming our child.

We are not suggesting you get drunk. We're saying to accept that this is a life-changing, stressful situation for both of you, and you'll need to find healthy ways to deal with it, communicate about it, and support each other.

One thing that helps is finding someone to talk with. It could be a therapist or just a good friend, but preferably it's someone with kids who has some age and wisdom on you. For me, it was my father at first. I remember his counsel to me on the day after I found out about the pregnancy went something like this: "Son, I can tell you one thing. As bad as this seems to you now, I can promise it will get better. Just like when things are great, that too isn't permanent. Life is a series of ups and downs, so try not to let yourself get too worked up about either of them."

After several months, although Mary and I were not getting along, I succeeded in getting some of my questions answered by talking with knowledgeable people such as other single parents and family lawyers. Getting questions answered helped settle my mind. But it was hard finding someone in my shoes. Most people I talked to were divorced and had a slightly different set of problems than I had. And the lawyers didn't give out much advice for free. This book would have been a great help to me back then.

As I contemplated my situation, I started to see that my life had become a bit boring at the time of the "surprise." I had been dating unsuccessfully through my twenties, and I was starting to think I would never find someone right for me. As I approached thirty, I figured there was a chance I would never have a child, which concerned me.

After more thought, I realized the surprise pregnancy had actually kick-started my dull life. It got me out of a rut, out of a repetitive "going through the motions" existence. My life suddenly had a purpose. Once I started to look at it that way, it didn't feel so bad anymore. I became excited about parenthood, but I still had to figure out how to get along with Mary better.

Jessica was also as shocked as could be when she found out she was pregnant with Bill's child. For years, doctors had told her that her unusually shaped uterus would make it difficult to conceive, so she told herself this pregnancy was a blessing (and it was!). But she was supporting herself on a nurse's salary, and she wondered whether they would give her paid time off for maternity leave. How would she afford a lawyer, which everyone said she would need? And a bigger apartment? Although she loved Bill at one time, she wasn't sure she should marry him. Jess had many sleepless nights but found comfort in talking through the issues with her sisters and mother.

For his part, Bill started out doing the right things, such as being supportive and trying to find a suitable living arrangement for the three of them. But money was tight for him too. He needed to get his finances in order before he could be the father he wanted to be.

Pregnancy doesn't wait for anyone to get anything in order. It marches on with a reasonably precise date in which you will need an apartment and some money in the bank for food, diapers, etc. Jess and Bill misunderstood each other on many issues during the pregnancy, and it took a terrible toll on their relationship. If they had communicated better at the time, if they had both read this book, then perhaps they would have avoided their nasty yearlong court battle.

Mary was also freaking out, as anyone would. I already mentioned her anxiety due to her church's position on premarital sex, but in a way, that was the least of her worries. She was living in Arizona when she found out she was pregnant, and her morning sickness during the first trimester was so bad that it landed her in the hospital with dehydration. After the hospital visit, she decided to move back east to live near her parents, which worked out well for me since I lived and worked on the East Coast too.

Once back east, she had to look for a job. Yes, there are laws on discriminating against expecting mothers, but good luck proving you were rejected for that reason. She scrambled to find employment before she started showing too much, eventually taking a position she didn't want but that at least provided some health benefits.

My relationship with Mary suffered terribly during the long-distance pregnancy. One big mistake I made was to get into long-winded email discussions with her when I should have just picked up the phone and talked to her. Emails and texts never convey the intended tone, and all too often, you may write something you regret or that gets misinterpreted. Additionally, anything you put in writing could be used against you if you end up in a courtroom (more on this in chapter 6). Don't make the same mistake I made; avoid emails and texts regarding emotional issues whenever a voice conversation is possible instead.

It's Harder on the Woman

It's important to emphasize to the male readers that whatever stress and anxiety they are feeling, the mother is feeling about ten times that amount. Maybe a hundred times.

After all, it is the mother who could be experiencing morning sickness, sometimes making it impossible to get through the workday. It's the mother whose body will soon be drastically changing shape and whose hormones might be spiking and crashing like a rollercoaster. It's the mother who must navigate judgmental friends, family, and employers, more so than the fathers. It's the mother who will be going on maternity leave, putting her career on hold for at least three months, whether she likes it or not. Paternity leave for fathers is becoming more typical but probably will never be as commonplace as maternity leave.

Fathers-to-be are well-advised to frequently and genuinely ask the mother how they are doing. How are they feeling? What do they need? What can you do for them? You might be surprised how far just showing some genuine compassion will go.

I did not do enough of this during Mary's pregnancy. Sure, I asked her how she felt, and I bought her a few gifts here and there, but I could have and should have been more sympathetic to what she was going through. Looking back, I can only wonder whether we could have avoided some of our differences if I had tried harder to show empathy during those first nine months.

Remember, guys, the mothers are the ones who will have to go through the agony of childbirth. They are the ones who live in constant fear of something going wrong with the baby growing inside of them. The constant fear of miscarriage. The constant fear of premature labor. They can't even sleep in certain positions without fear of harming the fetus inside of them—assuming they can sleep at all, given the discomfort of pregnancy.

Of course, men are concerned about these things, too, but guys should imagine how much more real it would be if the baby you were worried about was physically inside of you, 24/7. If you try to put yourself in the woman's shoes before every conversation, we promise you will find your relationship benefits.

Ask, Don't Tell

Early in Mary's pregnancy, I made a big mistake. We had a few preliminary discussions about challenging issues such as marriage and where to live, but everything was still very new and totally up in the air at that point.

Being the type A planner that I am, I took to my computer and started working out a baby plan. I started laying out all the pros and cons of various living arrangements. As I said before, I "calculated" that getting married right away would increase the odds of divorce early in the child's life, so I concluded we should wait on marriage.

I also came to other carefully considered conclusions about our living situation. For example, I calculated that Manhattan was way too expensive for Mary, even with my child support payments added to her salary. A quick search online for the prices of daycare and nannies in the city shocked me. Another quick search for apartments told me there was no way the three of us would be able to find suitable housing unless perhaps we all lived together, which I didn't think we were ready for.

All that figuring and calculating wasn't so bad on its own. It helped set my mind at ease to have a plan and get some answers.

My "big mistake" happened when I was out to dinner with Mary during the first trimester. I pulled out a printed copy of my plan at the candlelit table and proceeded to read it to her. It was really nothing more than a list of talking points. Seated across from her, I read off the paper in front of me. Bullet after bullet point of suggestions like "you and the baby should live near my parents' house in the suburbs . . . they can help you with childcare if you're close by . . . you can find local work as an assistant anywhere, but my job exists only in Manhattan . . . I can come to see you and the baby easily on the train . . . if we fall in love, we will get married someday, but there is no need for a shotgun wedding right now . . ."

Mary tried to interrupt me a few times, but I insisted, "Hold on, just let me finish. Hear me out." Of course, it wasn't much longer before she had stood up and stormed out of the restaurant in anger. A few minutes later, the food arrived, and I asked them to box it up. I felt all the eyeballs in the room staring at me, the jerk who just made his date cry and storm off before the food even arrived.

My bullet-point plan was well-intentioned and just meant to be a starting point of the discussion at dinner that night.

But all Mary heard was me telling her where to live and where to work, and that I wanted to just "visit" rather than be involved daily. She was pissed off and hurt, and rightfully so. I was a fool for thinking I could solve this baby like a financial equation or a jigsaw puzzle. Even worse, my insensitive delivery at the dinner table was utterly thoughtless, and Mary never forgot it.

At the very least, I should have started the discussion by asking her what she wanted rather than telling her what I thought would work best. Try not to make the same mistakes I did in this regard. Understand that no one wants to be told what will or should happen. Instead, ask your co-parent what they think will or will not work. Be diplomatic and sensitive here; show empathy. It's likely nothing will get solved in one sitting, no matter what, so don't even try for that.

And for God's sake, don't type up a plan and pull it out at the dinner table.

Type A or Type B?

If you are a type A person like me, you will need to fight the urge to plan out every detail of parenthood now, months before the birth. Neither of you knows what the situation will be after the baby is born or how your feelings about these things will change once you see the little person you've created and held them in your arms.

Besides, things change. You could get laid off from that job you thought was permanent. You might fall in love with your co-parent, or they may fall for someone other than you. You could end up with a special-needs child. Any of these things or a hundred others would require a different plan anyway. Remember, life makes a mockery of the best-laid plans.

Jess and I feel the best thing to do during the pregnancy is to discuss possibilities with your co-parent but leave the hard decisions until after the child arrives. This can be a challenge if you are a type A personality like me.

However, if you are a type B person, like Mary, you may have the opposite problem. You may be too laid-back; your aversion to planning and belief that everything will work out fine may cause your type A partner immense stress and is probably leading to arguments. Type A people just want to work out some answers or at least research some options. When Mary sometimes refused to discuss parenting arrangements during the pregnancy, it was hard for me. This led to a lot of long-winded emails by both of us that escalated into nasty arguments.

Let us also mention it's not always the man who is type A and the woman who is type B. Often, it's the woman who wants to plan the details and the man who is unwilling to commit or even discuss challenging subjects.

Neither type A or type B is right or wrong. They are just different. The key for both of you—and this advice holds in any relationship, not just co-parenting—is to understand what type of person you are and what type your partner is and then adjust your style accordingly.

Of course, you may get two parents of the same personality type, which will make things easier for you both. Jessica and Bill are close to the same personality types, meaning they both leaned closer to type B, but they are not extreme type Bs. They didn't get along for other reasons, but that's another story.

As I mentioned before, Mary is extremely type B. If she had been a little more willing to discuss practicalities and if I had been less insensitive and pushy about planning, then our relationship during the pregnancy could have been totally different. It took me way too long to figure out her brain works differently than mine.

It was only after years of parental counseling and legal mediation that Mary and I learned about our different personality types and how to bend to the other's style. After working with a parenting coordinator for a while, I think Mary learned the importance of timely communication and punctuality. Eventually, I accepted that she is not trying to piss me off when she delays a decision or is late for a meeting. Save yourself the stress, time, and money of counseling and just start from day one trying to understand the other person's personality type.

The next time you talk to your co-parent, try to show them empathy, try asking instead of telling, and try to see the world through their personality type. We promise you will get better results, you will sleep better at night, and in the long run, your child will benefit.

Everything Will Change

When the baby does arrive, everything will change, but it won't be all bad. You will see with your own eyes how helpless the child is. You will feel a deep connection and urge to take care of the child. If you are like most parents, it will be a positive experience, and you will have no problem sacrificing your time and money to support your little one in every way.

Things you used to care about, like TV and movies, sports and hobbies, bars and restaurants, will all fade into the background and seem trivial. Training to run that marathon suddenly might seem pointless or too time-consuming. A five-hour round of golf will become a rarity. Chores like cleaning out the garage will get moved to the back burner. Spending two hours a day at the gym will no longer be part of your routine.

This is parenthood, and if you don't know it already, you need to get it into your head as soon as possible that the child comes first. If you don't, you and your co-parent will never be able to function as a team. Any selfish requests will lead to arguments for sure, and you will not make the right decisions for your child.

We don't mean the child must consume your entire existence. Of course, you should make some time for *you*. One of the nice things about being a co-parent is that "you time" is built in automatically when the child is with the other parent.

Typically, co-parents exist somewhere between friends and hating each other's guts. Mary and I were closer to the hating end of that spectrum for a long time. So were Jessica and Bill—for the first year, at least. We are all in a better place now, in part because we all tried to put the children ahead of our personal, work, or social needs.

What we're getting at here is no matter where your relationship with your co-parent is, your conversations and interactions should focus on the child's needs, not yours. The discussion should always center on what's best for the baby rather than what's best for you.

Of course, this is precisely where many of the disagreements begin. Mom thinks Y is best for the child, while Dad thinks Z makes more sense. As long as the debate is between two parenting points of view, that's fine. You *should* debate the merits of Y vs. Z. What you want to avoid is any debate that pits your needs against the child's needs, because that will lead to a serious argument every time, and it will wreak havoc on your co-parenting relationship.

Co-Parenting Decision-Making

One of the first opportunities you will have to employ this idea of "child first" will be when you have to make the physical custody decision. Will you plan to share physical custody 50/50, or will one parent have primary physical custody and one parent be the "visiting" parent? A 50/50 arrangement means the child spends approximately equal time with each parent. This can work if the two adults live in the same immediate geographic location. But what if one of you lives in New York City and one resides in the DC area, as was the case for Mary and me when Kelly was born?

I would have liked to have 50/50 physical custody, but would that have been best for Kelly? Thinking it through, I realized Kelly could never spend half her time with me once she started attending school, but 50/50 probably was not going to work for her even before that age, given our distance. Furthermore, if I had had Kelly half the time, she would have been spending many of her days in NYC with a nanny or in a daycare center rather than with her mother. And she would have had to travel back and forth for many hours weekly. No good.

I didn't like the idea of being just a visiting parent, but unless Mary wanted to move to New York City, I had to accept that the best thing for our daughter was for Mary to have physical custody and me to have visiting rights. More on all this in chapter 6, but the point here is the decision was made based on Kelly's needs rather than what would have been my first preference.

Where to live and how to split the physical custody is one of the first decisions the two of you will need to make for your child. Of course, you must consider careers, because the child will need someone to support them financially. But you will also need to consider where the extended families live and whose home and schedule are more suitable for a child. If you are a road warrior traveling most of the month for business, you should not expect to take a young child (or any age child) with you. The child will be better off if you regularly visit in a consistent location than if you take them to a hotel month after month.

Physical custody may be the first big decision you make, but it certainly won't be the last. When will overnight visits with the visiting parent begin? What religion will the child be? Will you use breast milk or formula? Vaccinations? What happens if there is bad weather or the child is sick during your scheduled weekend? Will you agree to reschedule the visit, sacrifice the visit, or demand the visit happens no matter what? We will come back to each of these and other issues, but for now, our point is you should always make these decisions with the child's needs ahead of your own.

The trick is to be fair-minded and levelheaded, remembering the child has two parents and each must respect the other's thoughts on what constitutes "best for the child." It cannot be a one-way street. For example, if you think the child is too sick to travel for a visit, then you should probably allow a makeup visit. The child needs to spend time with both parents, and you should make sure that happens even if your calendar gets disrupted too.

High-Conflict Relationships and Parallel Parenting

The term *co-parenting* implies a situation where a mother and father attempt to cooperate for the child's sake. They don't always see eye to eye, but they put on a unified front for the child and do their best to respect each other's opinions and roles. If you are not in a happy marriage, then effective co-parenting is the next best thing for kids, and it's what we are striving for in this book.

However, some people cannot function as co-parents. They are so wrapped up in conflict with the other parent that they cannot even be in the same room together for more than a moment. They scream at each other on the phone and in front of the child. In some extreme cases, they make up horrible stories to get the other parent in trouble, either with the law or in the child's eyes.

The worst high-conflict cases involve parental alienation. We recently watched an eye-opening documentary called

Erasing Family (ErasingFamily.org), directed by Ginger Gentile, that addressed the growing problem of parental alienation and how the court system is not equipped to deal with it.

By some estimates, around 30% of all divorce cases fit into the "high-conflict" label, and we imagine the number is similar for baby-out-of-wedlock situations like yours. Endless lawsuits, badmouthing each other to the child, and withholding visitation or money are typical in these situations. Sooner or later, the child realizes what's going on. They tend to side with the healthier parent in the end, but years can go by in this horrible state if it's not dealt with effectively.

These high-conflict situations come in varying degrees, from low- to medium- to high-conflict. I think Mary and I were in a medium-conflict situation for the first few years. After a decade of duking it out and getting professional help, we are probably now down to a low-conflict or maybe even semi-effective co-parenting relationship, but just barely.

If you think your relationship might fall into this high-conflict bucket, we are sorry to say you have a hard road ahead. Most of this book will still apply to you, but some of our advice will need to be tweaked for the high-conflict situation you are in.

We urge readers in this boat to seek help from professionals in high-conflict custody situations. Our favorite high-conflict guru is Brook Olsen, who wrote *The Black Hole of High Conflict* and offers several levels of coaching services on HighConflict.net, including over one hundred free podcast episodes in which he dives deep into this subject. His work is excellent, and I wish I had discovered it sooner in my life because it would have saved me many years of heartache and perhaps thousands of dollars in legal bills.

We will mention some of Brook's specific strategies in later chapters, but the general idea is that high-conflict parents who cannot get along well enough to co-parent shouldn't even try. The better alternative for them is to "parallel parent." Parallel parenting is when you get an extremely detailed parenting plan and then live your life with your child as if the other parent was totally out of the picture. The three rules are "disengage, disengage, disengage," meaning you limit communication and do everything possible to avoid getting sucked into arguments, both legal and otherwise. It's not ideal, but it's better than living in a state of high conflict.

We are getting a little bit ahead of ourselves. The baby isn't even here yet, so let's get back to issues and questions you are facing now during the pregnancy. If you handle these well, you might be able to salvage your relationship before it turns into a high-conflict situation.

5 | Pregnancy and Infant Questions

This chapter's issues are not all-encompassing, nor are they a substitute for the latest medical advice. However, these topics were all areas of concern for Jessica and me during our first experiences with pregnancy, and we remember being overwhelmed with all the information out there. Our aim is to help you answer or at least start thinking about some of the health and parenting issues you will need to learn regarding your newborn.

Doctor Visits during Pregnancy

The first thing every expectant mother should do is schedule an appointment with an OB-GYN. Every woman is different, and depending on your body, age, and medical history, you may be considered a "high-risk" pregnancy. This is not as bad as it sounds. Jessica was considered high-risk during her first pregnancy because of her unusually shaped uterus. She was also considered high-risk when we had a child together years later simply because she was approaching forty years old. "High-risk" just means you will be watched more closely and have more checkups than a low-risk pregnancy.

Take your doctor's advice seriously. Five or ten decades ago, there was a decent chance either you or your baby would die in childbirth. Since then, one thing we humans have become pretty good at is having babies. The doctor knows what's best for you and your pregnancy. If they recommend a test or a pill, you should take it. If they tell you to avoid a particular food or activity, then avoid it. Don't listen to every old wives' tale or new fad you see on the internet. Choose a good doctor with solid experience and credentials and then respect their advice.

One issue that always worried me as a father before marriage was whether I should attend the doctor visits with Mary. Jessica also remembers having mixed feelings about Bill attending her appointments. This can be a problematic issue that you will need to discuss with your co-parent. On the one hand, the mother may be anxious and want the father there for support during the first doctor visit or two. On the other hand, she may not feel close enough with the father to invite him into her examination room. Our advice is that the father should ask (don't tell) the mother whether she would like him to be at the OB-GYN appointment, and if she says yes, then he should drop everything and make it happen.

There won't be any ultrasound images at the first doctor visit, but when it comes time to see your child in the womb for the first time, it is a magical experience for both parents. We recommend mothers invite the father to at least one of these ultrasound appointments. Even if you are not getting along very well, you should both try to make this happen. Sometimes the experience can help both of you put aside your differences and see that the little life you created is what matters most.

If the relationship is so sour that the mother doesn't want the father at any doctor appointments, then fathers need to respect that wish. Fathers have no legal right to attend, and like most other issues, insisting will get you nowhere.

Pregnancy Dos and Don'ts

There are piles of books and articles written on what pregnant women should and shouldn't put in their bodies. We don't intend to cover everything. Sometimes the medical advice changes over the years, and besides, there is just too much ground to cover.

The most straightforward rule of thumb for pregnant women is not to consume anything you wouldn't feed to a young child. Everything you put in your mouth, breathe in your lungs, and even rub on your skin can make its way into your child's fragile body.

Obviously, tobacco, alcohol, and drugs don't mix at all with pregnancy. Caffeine, processed deli meats, artificial sweeteners, and fish high in mercury, like tuna, are not recommended. If you get food poisoning, it can be dangerous for the fetus, so for that reason, they say to avoid unpasteurized milk and cheese, unwashed fruits, raw eggs, raw beef, raw shellfish, and sushi. Actually, sushi has both the food poisoning and the mercury risk. We have heard to stay away from licorice, soy, salt, excess peaches, soft cheeses, sprouts—the list goes on and changes occasionally, so ask your doctor for the most up-to-date information.

Besides what you eat, you also need to consider chemicals entering your body that may reach your baby through other means. Most mothers-to-be prefer to err on the side of caution, even if there is questionable evidence for some of these concerns. For example, Jessica was told to stay away from hair dye, teeth-whitening bleach, and even traditional nail polish. Apparently, they have "vegan" nail polish that is safe for pregnant mothers; perhaps there are safe alternatives to the other products as well.

While the list of "no-nos" is long, there is also a list of "should-do" recommendations. At the top of the list are pre-natal vitamins with folic acid, which experts say are important during the baby's early brain development. Again, ask your doctor for a vitamin recommendation. There are countless products marketed to help pregnant women be more com-fortable. Jessica loved Palmer's stretch mark cream, and when she was too big to sleep on her stomach, she got a full-length body pillow to help her sleep on her side. You can spend hours and thousands of dollars finding all sorts of pregnancy products. Fathers-to-be can earn some easy points by pur-chasing a few of these items as gifts.

Of course, there are countless books written for pregnant women. Jessica's favorite, which has stood the test of time and will give you straightforward answers, is *What to Expect When You're Expecting* by Heidi Murkoff. There are plenty of websites too. The trick is separating the quality informa-tion from the quackery, so be careful. One of the most popu-lar sites is Babycenter.com, which Mary, Jessica, and I found helpful. You give them your due date, and each week they send you an email with useful tips and information tailored to your baby's stage of development. The emails keep coming after birth until you turn them off, and the advice is designed for both mothers and fathers.

Fathers have it relatively easy during the pregnancy, to state the obvious. They get to keep on eating whatever they want and partying like it's 1999 without any consequences to the baby. But they don't get to experience the indescribable feeling of growing a person inside their body. All they can do is be supportive, buy a few gifts, and beyond that, maybe they can try to avoid indulging in some of those favorite no-no items in front of Mom.

What should fathers do if they see their pregnant co-parent doing something the doctors say not to do? Well, this is tricky. It's the woman's body, and you cannot dictate how they treat it. But the child inside is equally yours, and that child needs two parents looking after it, so you should not remain silent either.

The first thing would be to educate and inform the mom-to-be without accusing them of any wrongdoing or negligence. Something like, "Hey, I read this article about sushi. Take a look." Usually, that's all you will need to do, assuming the mother has concern for her unborn child. The vast majority of mothers are hypersensitive to ingesting anything that might cause harm, and a simple article is all it takes for them to err on the safe side.

Common sense goes a long way here too. A bite of sushi or an occasional small glass of wine won't do any damage, especially by the third trimester. However, if the mother-to-be is blatantly ignoring all the "rules" and perhaps even purposely attempting to sabotage the pregnancy, then I'm sorry to say that you have much bigger problems. If you are begging and pleading for your unborn child's well-being and Mom still won't listen to reason, then at that point, we think you would need to consult your lawyer. However, we are not sure they would be able to help much in that sort of situation.

Miscarriage and Premature Birth

If you Google "miscarriage," it will tell you that 80% of them happen in the first twenty weeks of pregnancy. Full term is thirty-nine to forty weeks, and anything under thirty-seven weeks is technically considered premature. Most doctors will say if you make it to thirty-four weeks, your baby is more or less out of the woods, although modern medicine does incredible things with premature babies born before thirty-four weeks nowadays.

Google goes on to say, "Among women who know they are pregnant, the miscarriage rate is roughly 10% to 20%, while rates among all fertilized zygotes (known and unknown) are around 30% to 50%. A 2012 review found the risk of miscarriage between 5 and 20 weeks to be from 11% to 22%." If it doesn't sound that high, remember 20% is one out of five.

Regarding premature births, about 10% of babies born in America are born before thirty-seven weeks of pregnancy, making them technically premature. In other words, miscarriage and premature birth are relatively common. They both happen often and frequently for no discernable reason. Sometimes it's just the luck of the draw.

But if you treat your body badly enough, it's possible to provoke a miscarriage or premature birth. Stress alone is probably a factor in both, but other genetic and environmental factors undoubtedly play a role too. Miscarriage is simply nature's way of ending pregnancies in which the fetus has a low chance of survival.

Miscarriage will affect you for the rest of your life, but it is nothing to beat yourself up about. Hopefully, you did the best you could during your pregnancy. You followed the doctor's orders. You took care of your body. You kept your stress levels down. Most of the time, there is no one to blame for a miscarriage except Mother Nature.

Signs of a miscarriage can be hard to describe and vary depending on how far along your pregnancy is, but they involve bleeding, cramping, and a general feeling of "something is wrong."

However, don't assume every drop of blood you see is an automatic miscarriage. "Spotting" (i.e., finding bloody spots in your underwear) is totally normal. Jessica and Mary both experienced some bleeding and fluid loss during their pregnancy. You should tell your doctor about spotting or fluid loss, but don't panic. Our sister-in-law went to the hospital with terrible bleeding once, midway through her pregnancy, and she did not lose the baby.

Miscarriage is a fear that mothers-to-be (and fathers) just have to learn to live with. And we can't say the fear goes away after twenty weeks. When you are a parent, you will be concerned about your child well after he is born, right up until the day you die. All you can really hope for is that you don't outlive your child. Outliving a child is a hardship we find difficult to fathom and wouldn't wish on our worst enemy.

Perhaps the most important thing that both co-parents can do during pregnancy, besides basic prenatal care described above, is to keep stress levels down. God forbid you get in an argument that turns into a screaming match that ends in a miscarriage or a very early premature birth. Don't let that be your story. Figure out how to get along with your co-parent and keep your stress levels down. Talk to a professional therapist to work out your issues in a healthy way. At a minimum, make sure to finish reading this book and ask your co-parent to read it, too, so you stop arguing over simple issues that you might not yet understand. In short, put your child first by avoiding heated arguments.

Ultrasounds and Genetic Testing

Every expectant mother will get at least two or three ultrasounds during the pregnancy and probably at least one maternal blood test. These are noninvasive screening tests that look for abnormalities in the fetus, and they are considered routine. In some low-risk cases, even the maternal blood tests are considered optional by the insurance company, which may require you to pay extra if you want the peace of mind the tests provide.

Routine ultrasounds will tell you the sex of the child, so if you want to be surprised, make sure to let the technician know in advance before they blurt it out. The doctor will look at the ultrasound for physical signs of possible genetic problems, such as fluid buildup on the back of the fetus's neck. If your ultrasound shows something suspicious, don't freak out just yet; these ultrasounds are often hard to read and inconclusive.

Mothers like Jessica, who are considered high-risk due to their age or other factors, will likely have more than three ultrasounds and more than one maternal blood test regardless of what the initial screening tests show.

If any of the routine screenings show developmental or genetic abnormalities, the doctor will likely encourage you to get further genetic testing. Some of them are considered invasive because they can involve a needle through the belly to extract amniotic fluid (amniocentesis) or a catheter through the cervix to gather cells from the placenta (chorionic villus sampling or CVS). These tests are not pleasant and do come with a low risk of miscarriage, so they are typically not used unless the doctor has good reason for concern and the mother is considering abortion due to possible severe genetic abnormalities.

Be sure to discuss the details with your doctor and fully understand what tests you are taking and what the results say. These tests evolve over the years, as do insurance company practices, so understand that just because someone you know did XYZ test a few years ago doesn't mean you should expect the same this year.

Umbilical Cord Blood Banks

Umbilical cord blood banks are another area that is evolving over time, so you should read up on the latest before making any decisions. Just make sure you find a neutral source of information because the internet is crawling with companies trying to sell their blood banking services. Some use scare tactics, preying on parents' fears. They cleverly disguise their websites to look like unbiased information sources when they are actually steering you right toward buying their product.

The basic idea of umbilical cord blood banks is to save blood or tissue from your newborn's umbilical cord at the time of birth just in case years later it may prove helpful in a medical situation for the child or a member of his family who has similar genetics. The cord blood is packed with stem cells, which can also be found in adult bone marrow. For various medical reasons, the umbilical cord stem cells are preferable to the bone marrow stem cells. Stem cells can theoretically treat some cancers, blood diseases like anemia, and some immune disorders. It is possible that years from now, science will unlock new uses for the stem cells that are currently only theoretical.

The problem is that it is unlikely your child's stem cells will ever be useful, at least with current technology. A study quoted on WebMD says the chance that a child will use their cord blood over their lifetime is between 1 in 400 and 1 in 200,000. One reason mentioned is that stored cord blood may be useful for only about 15 years.

Furthermore, cord blood is unlikely to be used by the donor if they develop a serious disease later in life because the genetic mutation that caused the disease probably also exists in the person's harvested stem cells. In these cases, the donor's cord blood containing his own stem cells cannot help him. However, if his sibling gets sick, then his stem cells might be able to help her. In some cases, a stranger's stem cells can help a person, but you always have compatibility risks with nonfamily donors. Siblings' blood is typically compatible.

There are basically three types of cord banks. Private cord banks charge a fee upfront and annually for storage, and it can be expensive. These are the websites we mentioned earlier that sometimes use scare tactics to get you to buy their service. If you want to make sure you have access to your child's stem cells for years to come, this option will ensure that. This option can make sense if you know your newborn has an older sibling with a genetic disorder.

Next, you have public cord banks that don't charge a fee. Anyone can donate cord blood to a public cord bank, and anyone can use the cord blood. It also may be used for research. Of course, you will not likely have access to your child's blood years from now if you donate it to a public cord bank. However, that is not necessarily a problem because, as previously mentioned, many diseases cannot be treated with a person's own stem cells anyway.

The third option is known as a direct-donation bank, which is a public bank that allows you to reserve your child's blood for your family. Typically, no fee is involved with this option, and it seems to be a nice compromise between the two other extremes.

With all three choices, you need to make arrangements in advance with your doctor or hospital so they know what to do on the day you deliver. Cord blood is the last thing you need to worry about when you are having a baby, and if you leave it to the last minute, it may be too late to choose any of the three options.

Should you do it? It depends on who you ask. When Mary was pregnant with Kelly, I did a little research and thought a private bank made sense as an insurance plan. However, Mary had dug deeper and was not fooled by the clever marketing from the private banks. She pointed out that the American Congress of Obstetricians and Gynecologists and the American Academy of Pediatrics don't recommend private banks unless there is an older sibling with a medical condition who could benefit. But they do recommend donating to a public bank. In the end, we didn't do either, mostly because our relationship was so rotten by the time the birth rolled around that we were just not communicating well. Jess and I suggest you read further on the topic and discuss your options with your co-parent and doctor.

Hospital vs. Alternative Birthing

Do a quick Google search and you will find a stat that reads like this: in the United States today, about seventeen women die in childbirth per 100,000 live births (0.017%). That's too many, but a century ago, more than six hundred women died per 100,000 births (0.6%). In the 1600s and 1700s, the death rate was twice that. By some estimates, between 1% and 1.5% of women giving birth died back then.

Looking up infant mortality rates, you will find similar trends. Recently in the United States, about six newborns died in childbirth per 1,000 live infant births (0.6%). In the year 1900, 165 newborns died in childbirth per 1,000 (16.5%).

Of course, the reason for these drastic improvements over the years is almost entirely due to advancements in hospital delivery room practices and newborn care. It is hard to appreciate this until you witness a birth yourself. In a hospital, there will be a whole team of nurses backing up your doctor in the delivery room. For a C-section, there are even more people and machinery involved.

When you give birth in a hospital, you can trust that they have seen it all, and they are prepared for almost everything that can go wrong. From the moment you walk in, your baby's heart rate and position in your belly are monitored. Sometimes the umbilical cord can wrap around the baby's neck, causing a major problem during labor if not addressed. Also, around 3 to 5% of babies become "breech," which means they are positioned with their heads upward instead of the more common and safer downward position. Breech babies are usually delivered cesarean section for safety reasons. Both of Jessica's babies were breech.

Immediately after the baby is born in a hospital, the nurses will suction all kinds of gunk out of his nose and mouth to help facilitate breathing. They will make sure the baby cries and breathes normally; if not, they will take drastic measures. They will carefully cut the cord and do a host of other things for both child and mother that need to be done, including taking care of any emergencies that might arise, like the near-death experience our friend's wife had.

She had a traditional vaginal birth in a hospital. The baby came out fine, and everything looked okay until they realized her uterus had come out along with the baby and she was bleeding uncontrollably. It was a rare emergency called an inverted uterus. She would have quickly bled out and died right there on the table except for the fact she was already in the hospital. She was saved and fully recovered in days.

Mary and I also had a scare when Kelly was born. Mary was a believer in some of the "natural birth" methods, and she wanted to avoid pain medicine, but thankfully she chose to deliver in a hospital. After a couple of hours of pain, Mary changed her mind about pain medicine and agreed to have an epidural, which is an injection of powerful anesthesia into the lower spine. She had been in labor for over twenty-four hours and was exhausted from pushing by the time I was called into the delivery room—which, by the way, was very big of her to allow, given we had not been getting along well at all during the pregnancy.

As the hours ticked by, the doctor kept telling us it wasn't going well, and he recommended she opt for a C-section, but

Mary was determined to push the baby out naturally. In some hospitals, they use large forceps to help extract the child, but instead, our doctor preferred the suction cup method. In this method, a soft suction cup on the end of a cord is attached to the baby's head, and the doctor pulls the child out of the birth canal. It didn't work. The doctor tried it three times. Each time, I watched him lean back with all his weight only to have the suction cup seal break, sending the doctor stumbling backward.

At this point, after hours of pushing and determining our child's life was in danger, the doctor made the executive decision to demand a C-section, whether Mary liked it or not. The hospital would allow only one person to accompany the mother in the operating room, and again Mary was gracious enough to allow me to be present. Within moments, we were hurried into an adjacent operating room, and in almost no time, Mary's belly was cut open and Kelly was delivered without any further complications. I cut the umbilical cord and held Kelly while Mary recovered with a quick and much-deserved power nap after they sewed her up.

Within an hour of her birth, Kelly was nursing in her mom's arms. If we had not been in the hospital, an emergency C-section would not have been possible, and the outcome would have been much different (worse).

About three days later, before leaving the hospital, we learned Kelly had developed a moderate case of jaundice. Jaundice is a common but serious issue for newborns if it's not addressed. The doctors required that Kelly stay in the hospital for an additional two days under ultraviolet light, which is the standard cure for jaundice. Again, thank goodness for modern medicine. We probably would not have even noticed the jaundice if we were not in the hospital.

The point of these frightening stories is to convey the risks you are taking for you and your child if you decide to deliver your baby outside of a hospital. There is a big industry out there that tries to sell mothers on "natural" delivery alternatives. Some use scare tactics to make pregnant women feel guilty if they use the traditional hospital system. They will tell you that hospitals somehow increase your risk or that using pain medicines will lead to autism or other nonsense.

Naturalists like to point out that women have given birth for thousands of years without hospitals, which is true, of course, but fails to mention the mother and infant death rates we discussed previously were much higher in the past. They push alternative birthing centers with a "homey" feel but usually not nearly the same emergency resources as a typical hospital. Some naturalists insist that home births, water births, midwives, and doulas are preferable alternatives to hospital births for various reasons. To deal with delivery pain without medication, they suggest yoga, breathing techniques, massage, visualization, acupuncture, even something called haptonomy, which involves the parents speaking to the unborn child in the womb during delivery to "ease the trauma" of childbirth.

As always, do your homework if you are considering an alternative birth plan outside of a hospital. Perhaps for some low-risk mothers, there are reasonable alternatives to a hospital birth. But to our thinking, the statistics overwhelmingly favor hospital births. Why push your odds of disaster back to the 1800s if you don't have to? Why bet your life and your child's life on the irrational insistence that your delivery will be perfect with no medical complications of any kind?

As with many of the topics in this section, the ultimate choice of where to give birth is the women's decision to make. Do yourself a favor: play it safe and stick with the hospital birth if possible.

C-Section vs. Natural Birth

There is not much to worry about here because most women will not have a choice between cesarean section and vaginal birth. Although this topic concerns only the woman, we include it and others like it so both parents understand the issues.

Traditional vaginal births typically involve two nights in the hospital and require fewer medical resources, so they are cheaper than C-sections, which usually demand four nights in the hospital and more medical staff and resources. For this reason, the insurance companies typically don't allow women to opt for a C-section unless there is a medical reason the doctor can point to.

If you are in a higher risk group like Jessica was due to her age or some other factor, then the doctor will either allow, recommend, or in some cases, demand a C-section delivery. If you find yourself with a choice, here are a few of the pros and cons of each to consider.

Vaginal birth is decidedly more "natural" and may have some built-in advantages for the child. Some researchers believe the baby benefits from an initial dose of good bacteria as they travel through the birth canal, which may boost their immune systems. It is also thought that the tight squeeze the baby experiences on the way out helps push out fluid in the newborn's lungs and airways.

There are some downsides to vaginal birth for the child as well. Due to the tight squeeze, some newborns come out with a cone-shaped head or even injured collarbones, although these are usually fixable. Breech babies are definitely at higher risk if born vaginally, as previously mentioned.

For the mother, a vaginal birth means a shorter hospital stay but also likely a more painful delivery and possible stretching or tearing of the vaginal tissue that, in some cases, may require stitches. Some research has found that vaginal births can lead to mothers having problems with incontinence later on.

For C-section births, mothers have a more extended hospital stay and overall recovery time. You will need someone to help you get around and care for the child over the first week or two because you will not be able to climb stairs or lift the baby for a while. While you have less pain on the delivery day than a vaginal birth, you will have more pain during the recovery week or two. Most women use some sort of prescription pain killer for at least a few days after a C-section.

C-section is a serious invasive surgery that carries added risks not seen with vaginal delivery. One study showed women are three times more likely to die during a C-section due to blood clots, infections, and other complications. However, the numbers are still very low, and there are certainly risks to vaginal childbirth, as we have touched on already. With a C-section, the abdominal muscles are cut open, and some women find it difficult to rebuild that muscle for months or even years. However, we were surprised to see how small the incision scar was on Jessica after her C-sections. It was only a few inches across and well below her belly button.

Once you have your first C-section, you will likely be advised to deliver future babies with C-section due to the weakened abdominal wall from your first one. Each subsequent C-section can add medical complications to the procedure. According to some studies, babies born by C-section may be more likely to have breathing problems and might be at a higher risk for stillbirth.

Jessica's first C-section was *not* uneventful. The doctor had difficulty and actually had to call out for help during the delivery because Adam's shoulder was stuck in an awkward position due to him being breech. When they finally got him out, he didn't breathe for a few seconds, giving everyone in the room a good panic attack. Drama aside, Jessica was thrilled when they told her she should do another C-section for her second child. Apart from all the other reasons described above, she loved having a date certain on the calendar when she knew she would be delivering.

Approximately 30% of childbirths in America are performed via C-section. The decision will largely depend on your medical condition and your doctor's advice. If you have a choice to make, Jess would recommend a C-section every day of the week and twice on Sundays—although to be fair, she never delivered vaginally.

Vaccinations

Vaccinations are a hot-button topic, even though Jess and I believe they really shouldn't be. Mary has always been emotional about vaccination, feeling that it is unnatural to inject a dead virus into your body. She is not alone; a number of people believe vaccines are a scam created by Big Pharma to make money, both by selling the vaccine and planting the seeds of future illness in the population. Anti-vaxxers blame everything from autism to cancer on trace ingredients like mercury in some vaccines.

The COVID-19 vaccines are a different story. At the time of this writing, these vaccines are brand new, and so it is impossible to know the long-term effects they might have until years go by. We understand how someone might be concerned about unknown side effects from a COVID-19 shot. However, our discussion here refers to vaccines that children have received for decades for diseases like polio, hepatitis B, and the annual influenza shot. Admittedly, we are not doctors or scientists, and we may be wrong, but Jess and I feel the numbers speak for themselves on those vaccines that have stood the test of time.

Mary has typically refused to get Kelly a yearly influenza shot on the theory that it does more harm than good, and we have argued about it annually. But even Mary agreed to get Kelly vaccinated over her first two years for the fourteen or so vaccinations that the doctors recommended and a few more that were scheduled for the years after that. Major diseases like polio have been all but eradicated with the help of vaccines. In many places in America, it is considered illegal and akin to child endangerment if you don't get your infant vaccinated against the most serious diseases.

It's hard to pinpoint why some people are so fearful of vaccination when it is such a modern medical marvel. Vaccination has literally saved *billions* of lives since it was first invented about a hundred years ago. Some celebrities have undoubtedly added to the spread of misinformation. Mothers become fearful their child will be in the one in a gazillion that has an adverse reaction to the shot, leaving their child paralyzed or worse. Sometimes the idea you could cause your child harm is so powerful that it leads you to ignore the numbers.

You can Google the numbers or look them up at the CDC website. Approximately one in a million children have an adverse reaction to vaccinations. The exact figures vary depending on which vaccine you're talking about. But in all cases, the chances of contracting an illness if you are not vaccinated is higher than the chances of an adverse reaction to the vaccination.

Furthermore, there is a network effect at work here. The population as a whole is definitely better off when the vast majority get vaccinated. You may think your child is safe because everyone else is vaccinated. However, there have been many outbreaks over the years of what should be "dead" or dormant diseases due to small pockets of the population that refuse to get vaccinated.

Jess and I strongly believe you should get your baby's vaccinations done on the schedule that your doctor recommends. You owe it to the rest of the population, but more importantly, you owe it to your child to play the odds rather than your emotions.

SIDS and Sleep Training

Sudden Infant Death Syndrome (aka SIDS or crib death) is the mysterious sudden death of healthy infants under age twelve months, typically at night. While the SIDS rate has dropped dramatically in recent decades, it still kills about 2,500 infants per year in the United States, according to Google. SIDS is every parent's nightmare.

With SIDS, there are no warning signs. Most cases involve perfectly healthy babies who die in almost the same position they were left in. In other words, it is not because they rolled over and suffocated. It seems to be some failure of the child's involuntary circulatory system to function. While the causes are not widely understood, there appears to be one simple best practice that will lower your child's risk of SIDS.

The one all-important rule to avoid SIDS is to put your child to sleep flat on his back in a crib without any loose blankets. In the past, it was noted that many SIDS cases involved children sleeping on their stomachs, which some have theorized make it more likely they will rebreathe exhaled carbon dioxide, which could perhaps contribute to SIDS.

Some studies have shown that a pacifier might reduce the risk of SIDS, perhaps because it might help prevent your child's internal systems from "freezing up" during sleep. The most statistically significant risk of SIDS is your child's age; most cases occur between one and four months old.

While suffocation is not the same thing as SIDS, the result is the same. Co-sleeping in the same bed is a terrible mistake because hundreds of exhausted parents end up rolling over on their child every year, suffocating them. Blankets and pillows in the crib are another big no-no. Your infant doesn't need either, and the chance that they could restrict his airflow is just too great.

One of the first things you will learn as a new parent is that your newborn loves to be "swaddled," which means wrapping him up snugly in cloth. This gives him the familiar feeling of being secure in the womb. At first, he will wake up every few hours to feed, but the wake-up frequency will decrease over time.

There is no reason your infant cannot learn to sleep through the night, starting at around three or four months, if you help him learn how. One smart recommendation is to put him down in his crib before he falls asleep so he learns to drift off on his own without someone comforting him. This will require that you don't come running in every time you hear him whimper on your baby monitor.

A tool Jessica and I had great success using was an infant sleepsuit called the Baby Merlin's Magic Sleepsuit, which is designed to be used starting at age three months. For whatever reason, both of Jessica's children loved sleeping in this thing. By age four months, they were sleeping through the night on their own.

Sleeping through the night is perhaps the most critical skill a parent can teach an infant. The child needs to learn to fall asleep on his own so if he wakes up during the night, he can soothe himself back to sleep. It is also important so the parents can get back to a regular night's sleep after a few months of waking every few hours to feed the baby. There are all sorts of books and methods out there you can read about getting your child to sleep through the night. Take the time to read them and form a plan that works well for you and your co-parent, who will have the child overnight sooner or later.

Breastfeeding

Mary, Jessica, and I are all big believers in breast milk. Study after study points to the benefits to the child. For example, breast milk contains antibodies and lowers the risk of asthma, allergies, ear infections, and respiratory illness. Mothers will tell you what an incredible emotional bond it creates, which can't be a bad thing. It is even thought to promote the child's brain development. Who knows what other benefits Mother Nature built into breast milk?

However, as with many things in life and parenting, you must play the hand you are dealt, and sometimes breastfeeding just doesn't work. Some babies never learn to latch on to the mother's nipple, and some nipples are just too small or even inverted, making it especially challenging. Other mothers are physically able to nurse, but employment or other demands make it impossible.

Nursing a baby seems simple until you try to do it for the first time. There is often someone called a lactation consultant who floats around the hospital maternity ward, teaching new mothers how to nurse. This speaks to the challenge it can present but also to the importance the medical profession puts on breast milk. After you leave the hospital, there are support groups of nursing mothers that some mothers find helpful to join.

Nursing can feel like a full-time job for the mother. At times it will seem like the baby just wants to suck 24/7, and at other times it's a challenge to empty your breastmilk before your chest feels like it's going to explode. Often nipples get chapped and sore, and God forbid you get a lactation mastitis, which is a painful nipple infection when bacteria from the baby's mouth enter the breast ducts.

Nursing is especially tricky if the mother must return to employment early on. Pumping your milk so other caregivers can feed your baby sounds easy, but in reality, pumping can be more difficult and time-consuming than actually nursing the baby. Jessica tried a few different expensive breast pump models with little success until she discovered the trick of pumping milk from one breast while the baby nursed on the other breast. Apparently, when the baby is attached to one nipple, it fools the other nipple into opening up. She also found a simple suction cup pump called the Haakaa Pump worked as well for her as the expensive electronic models. Even if you are not returning to work anytime soon, storing breast milk will come in handy when a babysitter or co-parent is caring for the child. Just make sure you freeze it immediately, because it goes bad after a couple of days in the refrigerator.

Because it is so demanding and, in some cases, impossible to nurse, many children are raised on formula alone, and there is nothing wrong with that. Millions of kids do just fine on formula. Our suggestion is to give nursing your best effort, shooting for at least three to six months of breastfeeding. If you can make it longer, that's great, but if not, don't beat yourself up too much.

Jessica nursed our son until age six months and was thrilled to cut it off at that point, feeling she had done her duty. Mary made it much longer than that. She nursed our daughter, Kelly, every day of her life, except on days when she was visiting me, until her *fourth* birthday. Yes, four years old! I wouldn't believe it if I didn't see it for myself year after year.

Postpartum Depression and Other Issues

Nine months of pregnancy, followed by the stresses of childbirth and all the challenges that come with caring for a newborn, can really take a toll on mothers. Fathers are wise to be sympathetic, understanding, and helpful during the weeks and even months after childbirth, which is known as the postpartum period.

There is a long list of physical issues that women can face after childbirth, including various infections, vaginal bleeding or discharge, breast and nursing problems, hemorrhoids, constipation—the list goes on and on. Some issues arise on the day of birth, and others can take months to develop. There are plenty of medical resources out there to help you deal with these issues, and some can be serious, so make sure to communicate problems to your doctor.

According to CDC research, one of the most common postpartum issues is depression, which affects about one out of nine new mothers. It is different from "baby blues," which usually passes a few days after birth as hormones fluctuate back toward normal. The body goes through such a wild ride during and after the pregnancy that sometimes it kicks off a deep depression spell that can last for weeks or even months.

For women experiencing severe postpartum depression, it can be quite debilitating. In some extreme cases, they may even have thoughts or fears that they will hurt their baby. Mary's mother told me that although she had four kids, it was after only one of them that she experienced terrible postpartum depression. She said it got so bad that she felt she was hallucinating some of the time.

The good news is that like all depressions, postpartum depression is treatable if you recognize the signs and seek help. Fathers should try to keep an eye out for it and be as understanding and helpful as possible without overstepping their role as a co-parent, which, of course, is different from a husband. It can be a tight line to walk during a delicate time.

It can also be hard to discuss or negotiate any kind of longer-term custody or visitation schedule with a mother who is going through postpartum depression or other post-birth issues. In my case, I was anxious to get the legal ball rolling, but I just couldn't bring myself to have that conversation with Mary for the first month of Kelly's life. Although Mary didn't have any significant postpartum issues that I was aware of, it just felt like the first few weeks was the wrong time to start a legal negotiation.

When we finally did have that talk, it didn't go very well. I can only imagine how difficult the conversation would be if Mom were dealing with one or more postpartum issues. Thinking back on it now, I wonder if maybe Mary *was* going through a postpartum issue and I was too obtuse to realize it. Anyway, if you can wait a bit, it is probably better for both parties' interests if you can delay the legal discussions until everyone's head is in the right place. However, you don't want to wait too long, because the legal process can take over a year. We will discuss our recommended timeline more thoroughly in the next chapter.

Substance Abuse

A word about substance abuse. If you have a substance abuse problem—drugs, alcohol, opioids, whatever—you can be sure it will get in the way of your parenting relationship with your child and your relationship with your co-parent. Aside from all the obvious challenges addiction will cause in your life, be aware that your co-parent will use it against you every chance they get if you are locked in a nasty legal battle with them. The court does not look kindly on someone with DUIs on their record or a history of drug abuse.

It must be said that if you cannot control your drug or alcohol use, then perhaps your co-parent is right to try to protect the child from your problems. There are plenty of horror stories of loving parents who unwittingly kill their children in car accidents or worse while under the influence of one thing or another.

Jess and I have a sister-in-law whose sister has a terrible drug addiction. She loves her child, but she just couldn't quit the drugs despite multiple trips to rehab. One day, the police found her passed out in the driver's seat of her parked car with a needle in her arm and her two-year-old in the back seat, crying, dirty diaper, no shirt, etc. From that point on, the court took away her unsupervised visitation rights. Her son now lives with his father and his grandparents.

Unfortunately, it has now been years since she has seen her son because she still can't clean her life up even to attend an occasional supervised visit. It's such a sad situation but all too common. The poor kid has been told for six years now that his mother is "sick but getting better somewhere far away." As he becomes a teenager, he will figure out the truth sooner or later. Hopefully, she recovers eventually, but they will never get the lost years back.

Even if you are not shooting up heroin, you can be sure your bad habits will be discussed if there is a court battle over custody or visitation. In some nasty cases, a co-parent will paint you as a danger to your child even if you are not. Casual drugs, alcohol, smoking marijuana, and even cigarettes nowadays are frowned on in most jurisdictions.

The fact is you cannot be a good parent if you have a substance abuse problem, so if you have one, then take the steps now, during the pregnancy, to get cleaned up. There are plenty of resources to help you, such as Samhsa.gov, AA.org, NA.org, and SmartRecovery.org.

And if you don't have a problem but your co-parent might think you do, then be aware the courts can order drug tests, sometimes on the spot with little or no warning, if one parent makes a convincing argument that the child is in danger. Do your best not to give your co-parent anything to worry about or use against you. The best advice is to avoid anything questionable, especially when spending time with your co-parent or child.

Parenting Styles

You will probably not know what kind of parent you will be until the child arrives and you experience parenthood for yourself, which is fine. As my cousin told me before Kelly was born, "Don't worry so much. All they really need is love."

However, it doesn't hurt to read up on various styles and keep an open mind. There is no reason you need to sign up for one style and stick with it forever, but on the other hand, it is good to become informed of the various schools of thought.

Some parents latch on to one type of parenting that feels right to them. Mary knew before Kelly was born that she wanted to practice a style called "attachment parenting." There are entire books written on attachment parenting and every other parenting type, so we won't try to cover them all here.

While this book does not attempt to cover parenting styles, it does aim to help your relationship with your co-parent. We mention attachment parenting only because we have experience with it. It will serve as an excellent example of how co-parents must consider each other when making parenting decisions if they want a positive relationship.

The gist of attachment parenting is you keep the child attached to the mother physically and emotionally, around the clock. You never, ever let the child cry for more than a few seconds. You respond to his every whimper with whatever he craves (usually a breast). Breastfeeding is an integral part of attachment parenting, as is co-sleeping in the same bed and keeping mother and child in constant contact. The theory is that the mother-child bond is of utmost importance to the child's development.

You might be thinking, *Well, that doesn't sound like a great parenting style if you are not married*. You would be correct. It caused a boatload of problems for Mary and me. Attachment parenting is also problematic for mothers who plan to return to work after a few months of maternity leave, because the infant has never learned to cope without their mother when it's time for daycare to begin. Furthermore, mothers cannot breastfeed around the clock if they are at work.

Since attachment parenting demanded breastfeeding literally whenever the child "asked" for it, Mary felt she needed to be nearby, ready to nurse 24/7. She was unwilling to pump breast milk into a bottle for me or for anyone else to feed Kelly. The attachment parenting thinking is that it is not just the milk that matters but also the connection to the mother's skin and strengthening the emotional bond that are equally important.

There is also supposedly a concern about "nipple confusion," whereby the child learning to breastfeed might get confused early in the learning process if you flip back and forth between a real and fake nipple. Jessica and I believe this is a valid concern only in the first few weeks of nursing, but after that, sucking on a nipple is like riding a bike. Mary disagreed, and therefore I never got to feed Kelly with a bottle as an infant. Years later, I did regularly bottle feed my son, and he never had any problems with nipple confusion.

Furthermore, Mary was adamantly against the use of even a pacifier (again, possible nipple confusion), leaving me very little chance of soothing Kelly when she was fussy as an infant. Mary also slept in the same bed as Kelly from an early age and for many years to come, despite the well-known dangers of sleeping with an infant (you might roll over and suffocate them), because this was another core tenant of attachment parenting. Mary felt this attachment parenting style, which included the co-sleeping practice and 24/7 nursing, was a valid reason why I should wait *years* before having unsupervised or overnight visits with Kelly.

As you can imagine, this was a significant source of stress and conflict between Mary and me early in Kelly's life. On the one hand, I was all for breast milk, and I was thrilled Mary was forming a strong mother/daughter bond with Kelly. But on the other hand, I wanted to bond with Kelly too. If I couldn't feed her a bottle or even soothe her with a pacifier, then it might be difficult to bond during my relatively short weekend visits. I worried that if I weren't bonding with her during the brief supervised visits in Mary's house, how would we ever progress to longer, unsupervised visits?

Wait, wait, wait! Didn't we just tell you in the last chapter to put your selfish needs aside and do what's best for the child? Well, yes, and we also said that is where most of your arguments will stem from. You will not always agree with your co-parent on what is "best" for the baby.

Mary had read about many different parenting styles during her pregnancy, and she concluded attachment parenting was the right fit for her. She didn't need to return to work immediately, and after all, I was living relatively far away, so she didn't think there was any reason Kelly should have overnight visits with me for several *years*. Therefore, she went all in on the attachment parenting philosophy. I believe this led her to decide she would fight tooth and nail in the courts to limit my unsupervised and especially my overnight visits, which you will hear more about in the next chapter.

I, too, had done some reading during Mary's pregnancy. My conclusion was that the best parenting style for any child, but especially for Kelly since she had co-parents who were geographically separated, was more akin to the one described in *Eat, Sleep, Poop: A Common Sense Guide to Your Baby's First Year* by Dr. Scott W. Cohen. The author is a pediatrician (and a parent) who believes it is the parents' job to help the child get the basics right, like eating, sleeping, and pooping, and then the rest will fall into place. Dr. Cohen's book cuts through much of the fear and nonsense out there, and his approach leads to practical, healthy results for your child, in our opinion.

Dr. Cohen's approach in *Eat, Sleep, Poop* also happens to work much better for a child raised by co-parents. In some ways, it is an anti–attachment parenting style. It is all about doing things that work—for example, helping your child learn how to sleep through the night on his own rather than needing a breast every few hours to fall back asleep. There are pages written about sleeping in this book, and many others agree with Dr. Cohen, but the basic idea is you can teach your child as early as three months old to fall asleep on his own and stay asleep for many hours. Far from being cruel or unloving, teaching your child how to sleep on his own is one of the best gifts you can give him. Of course, if your child sleeps through the night, then you will, too, leaving you to be at your best during the day.

We have two quick anecdotes to drive home this discussion before we move on. As I mentioned, Kelly and Mary had co-slept in the same bed for over a year by the time I had my first overnight visit with Kelly. Until then, I believe Kelly had never slept more than about four hours at a time next to her mom without waking up to nurse. I was nervous about her first overnight visit with me when Kelly would be in a crib all by herself for the first time. I had a plan from the books I read to help her fall asleep on her own by letting her "cry it out" more or less. On the night in question, I put her down at around eight o'clock in her crib all by herself. I left the room, planning to return every ten minutes or so to reassure her if she was crying. She whimpered for about five minutes. Then she slept for eleven hours straight! I was in shock but also so relieved. I can only imagine how great a full night's sleep must have felt to Kelly for the first time in her life at age fourteen months.

Contrast Kelly to Jessica's first son, Adam, and our recent child, Kevin. Adam and Kevin were raised in more of the

Eat, Sleep, Poop style, in part because Jessica had to go back to work after a few months but also because it just made more sense to her and seemed better for her boys. Adam and Kevin were both sleeping through the night, starting at age three or four months. They both breastfed for the first six months, but Jess pumped milk daily to send to daycare or let someone else like me help with the feeding. Nipple confusion never got in the way, and although they both used a pacifier occasionally, they never got "addicted" to it as some kids do.

Now, the real question would be which child is better off, the one who was raised by attachment parenting or the ones raised by more practical styles like those described in *Eat, Sleep, Poop*? What about other styles not mentioned here? Our answer is that in the long run, it didn't matter that much, at least not to the kids.

Kelly, Adam, and Kevin have all turned out to be healthy, smart, and emotionally well-adjusted kids. Of course, they each have their challenges, but I cannot say that either attachment parenting or Dr. Cohen's *Eat, Sleep, Poop* styles made any lasting difference. All the children have strong bonds and healthy relationships with their respective parents.

But we are not saying the different styles had no consequences. Jessica and Bill had a rough first year together, but it had nothing to do with parenting styles. In other words, the practical *Eat, Sleep, Poop* style didn't produce any problems for them. On the other hand, Mary and I had a disastrous first five years, including terrible legal actions every year, in large part, I would argue, due to Mary's insistence on extreme attachment parenting.

Research shows the quality of co-parenting has a significant impact on children's emotional wellbeing. According to the LMFTs (Licensed Marriage and Family Therapists) we know, co-parental conflict can lead to the development of emotional and behavioral problems in your child, such as:

- Lower self-esteem
- Difficulty forming healthy adult relationships
- Increased risk of substance abuse/addiction
- Difficulty communicating
- Poor emotional regulation
- Personality disorders
- Poor academic performance
- Increased risk of anxiety, depression, and suicidal ideation

Obviously, parenting styles matter also, but Jess and I believe that if you have to choose between your preferred parenting style and a healthy co-parenting relationship, the co-parenting relationship should take priority. In other words, having a dysfunctional co-parenting relationship is likely to negatively impact your child more than a perfect parenting style will help them.

Each mother and father reading this book will need to decide what sort of parent they want to be. There are lots of styles beyond the two types we reviewed here. We are not saying which parenting styles are good or bad for the child. We are saying that before you decided to go all-in on one particular type, make sure you consider your co-parent in the decision. Of course, you have to do what's right for you at the end of the day. Just don't make the mistake Mary did of disregarding the other co-parent's wishes because you're not married. Co-parent means just what it says: two people count.

With that thought in mind, now let's dig into the meat of this book: legal issues.

6 | Legal Questions

This is the chapter that can really save you some money. Years ago, Jess and I each spent close to $400 an hour for lawyers to explain these issues to us. Even though your attorney will know the law, they are not always the best teachers. Sometimes they are so "in the weeds" that it might be hard for them to relate to someone who has never been through litigation before. This dynamic can make it challenging to learn the basics from your attorney, which results in more follow-up questions and higher legal bills.

Furthermore, be aware that some attorneys are more interested in increasing their billable hours than doing what's best for you. The sneaky ones are great at learning your trigger points, and they know how to nudge you along from one billable hour to the next. For example, when your co-parent breaks a rule or provokes you somehow, these attorneys will push you to "respond" with an expensive letter or legal action even when none is needed. The worst of them will encourage you to fight for months for something you don't have any chance of winning in trial.

Conversely, the best lawyers will always push you toward compromise and a legal settlement. They know the courtroom is never the best result for anyone. Trustworthy attorneys will tell you, "No need to respond to that," at least *some* of the time.

I had a great attorney, as defined above. Still, by the time I was done with my "education," I had spent $165,000 in legal bills over five years. Approximately $60,000 of it was on the initial custody battle with Mary, which ended around my daughter's first birthday. The rest was spent on subsequent legal actions with her over the next few years. Jessica spent $30,000 on her custody disagreement with Bill, and she didn't go to trial either. Both of us would have spent a lot more if we had ever gone to trial, and it would have been a lot less if we had read this book first.

Fear not. By the end of this chapter, you will have a firm grasp of the legal issues you need to understand. We can't answer everything, and we are certainly not a substitute for a competent attorney, but at least you won't need to pay your lawyer to explain the basics. If you can get your co-parent to read this book, then you will see even more benefits from cooperation, and you won't spend anything near what we spent on legal bills.

If you are trapped in a high-conflict situation, you will want some added coaching to survive it. There is a whole cottage industry out there helping parents and divorcees navigate high-conflict situations, and they are worth investing your time and money on if your co-parent is just totally impossible to work with. For starters, pick up a book or listen to a podcast on the subject (see our website for suggestions: BabyOutOfWedlock. com). These resources cost you nothing but should help you begin to cope with your difficult situation.

If the free resources are not enough, coaches like Brook Olsen (HighConflict.net) can help people in high-conflict situations. They take on clients for one-on-one coaching, which functions as something between legal advice and therapy. They understand family law, but unlike attorneys, they are trained to help you deal with the emotional realities of a nasty legal battle while teaching you how to limit the amount of money you throw down the litigation drain.

And finally, for many people, talking with a great therapist is the solution for dealing with the unbelievably frustrating experience that co-parenting and the family law court system can be. If you are in a high-conflict situation, make sure to seek help in one form or another. You cannot do it effectively on your own, especially if this is your first experience with a custody battle.

But, even if you are not in a high-conflict situation, you still have to watch out for common mistakes that can send you into a downward spiral. One of the biggest problems both Jessica and I had was our co-parents were either ignoring legal advice (in Mary's case) or receiving bad legal advice (in Bill's case), leading to all sorts of significant difficulties. If you are both mature and well-informed, there really shouldn't be any need for a long or expensive legal battle. We would even go as far as to say that if you are both reasonable people who read this chapter, then there shouldn't be any legal battle at all.

Pregnancy Discrimination and Maternity Leave

Before we jump into the good stuff, we should make sure you know there are laws out the wazoo protecting pregnant employees and pregnant job hunters. The Pregnancy Discrimination Act of 1978 is a federal statute that forbids discrimination based on pregnancy concerning any aspect of employment, including hiring, firing, pay, job assignments, promotions, layoff, training, fringe benefits, and any other terms of employment for companies with fifteen or more employees.

A potential employer cannot ask you if you are pregnant or plan to have children at the interview or anytime after your employment begins. You cannot be fired for taking sick days while you're pregnant, and in many places, local laws offer even more protection. For example, New York City requires employers to "provide reasonable accommodations" for pregnancy and childbirth, such as minor changes to work schedules, dress codes, and additional break time, especially for nursing mothers who need to pump breast milk every few hours during the workday.

The Federal Family and Medical Leave Act of 1993 requires employers to offer up to twelve weeks of *unpaid* leave per year for parental and medical-related reasons but only for companies with over fifty employees and only if you have worked with the company for at least 1,250 hours over twelve months. Again, many states and cities offer even more protection, and the trend is in the direction of more robust offerings for parents. The state of New York now requires employers to offer ten weeks *paid* family leave, and in many places, the rules are starting to provide the same benefits for fathers and same-sex couples as they do for mothers. A quick Google search should tell you the laws in your state and locality.

Unfortunately, despite all the laws, there are still plenty of discriminatory or just ignorant employers out there that don't follow the rules. And, even if you sue for discrimination and win, you can bet there will be repercussions, especially if you want to stay with the company you are accusing or if you work in a small professional field. Word travels, and even confidential settlements have a way of marking you as a troublemaker. This is not fair or right, but it's just the world we live in, so you must think carefully about the pros and cons before you take action against an employer who discriminates against you.

In the meantime, while you consider your options, try to gather as much evidence as you can of the discrimination. Write down every instance and detail in a journal and communicate in writing with your employer whenever possible so there is a record of evidence other than just your word against theirs. You usually don't need to have direct, "smoking gun" evidence to win. Circumstantial evidence can be enough. For instance, if you have stellar reviews for five years, then you get a terrible review for no reason right after announcing your pregnancy, that would be a powerful piece of evidence (from The Spiggle Law Firm, Spigglelaw.com).

If you find yourself discriminated against due to pregnancy or maternity leave and want to take action, you will need to find a good local lawyer to walk you through it. You cannot wait very long because, in many cases, the statute of limitations is only 180 days. The laws vary widely from place to place, and there are exceptions you may not be aware of. For example, very small businesses may not have the same requirements as larger ones. Don't try to solve this problem on your own.

Okay, now back to the custody battle information.

Finding a Good Family Law Attorney in the Right Location

The first thing to know about family law and custody litigation is state laws almost entirely dictate it. There are some commonalities between many states but also a lot of differences, so you will need first to determine the jurisdiction (i.e., which state applies to your case).

This is straightforward if both co-parents and the child live in the same state. But what if Mom lives in Philadelphia and Dad lives just over the bridge in New Jersey, as was the case for Jessica and Bill? Mary and I had an even trickier situation that required some research to figure out.

Mary and I had initially met and dated when she lived in New York City. When she became pregnant, I was still living and working there, but she had moved to Arizona the previous year. She technically still had a NYC apartment lease in her name, but she had sublet it out to a friend while she was away. She got pregnant on a short visit back to New York. Was she a New York resident or Arizonian? I wasn't sure, legally speaking.

She returned to Arizona for her first trimester, where she experienced terrible morning sickness that landed her in the hospital due to dehydration. After that experience, she moved back home with her parents in the Washington, DC, suburbs in Maryland. During the pregnancy, I did a couple of legal consultations with lawyers in New York, and they advised me that if the baby was born in Maryland and the mother and child were living there, then Maryland law would dictate, not New York. I learned the state where mother and baby resided would be the state whose laws applied to my custody agreement (battle).

So, I asked the New York lawyers to recommend an attorney in Maryland, and they gave me a few names. After speaking to them on the phone, I narrowed down my list to two, and I arranged to meet them in person. This proved to be very important. One of the lawyers on my shortlist seemed very slow-witted and generally "out to lunch" during my face-to-face meeting. I found out months later he was closing his practice due to the onset of Alzheimer's disease.

But the other meeting was a success and thus began a very long and expensive relationship with one of the best family lawyers in Maryland. She had an almost comically perfect name for an attorney; I don't want to use it here, so I'll call her Mrs. Big instead.

During the pregnancy and immediately after the birth, Mary claimed she did not intend to live in Maryland for long. Typically this threat would come out amid a heated argument, so I never knew whether she was serious or just trying to scare me. The destination she usually mentioned was Arizona or California, and that would have presented me with the added challenge of finding a lawyer in a new state and learning a whole new set of rules.

Lucky for me, she never actually moved, and therefore most of my family law experience is with Maryland law. However, Jessica made her custody arrangement with Bill in Pennsylvania, so we have experience there too. Add in my knowledge of New York law, and that gives us enough perspective to understand which kinds of rules vary from state to state and which don't; however, we stress that you must speak with your attorney about your specific circumstances.

Once you figure out the right state, the next thing to think about is the locality. While technically any attorney licensed in your state can represent you, it helps to find someone with local knowledge.

Mrs. Big was well-known in the local Maryland community where she practiced and where Mary lived when Kelly was born. During several trips to the courthouse with her for various hearings, I noticed that she knew all the clerks and bailiffs passing by in the halls. She knew the judges and their personalities, as well as the character and reputations of other local lawyers, including Mary's legal counsel. She knew how judges had ruled in the past and which mediators would be a good fit for Mary and me and which would be a waste of time—or worse, unfair to me because of whatever bias they had.

If your lawyer is in the right state but doesn't typically practice in the jurisdiction you need, will she be as effective as a local on their home turf? Furthermore, do you want her billing you for the many hours it takes her to drive back and forth to a long-distance courthouse? For these reasons, ideally, you want to find a lawyer who is in the right state *and* the right locality.

We will cover the consequences of moving across the state or the country in another section, so we don't want to get into that just yet. But what if one co-parent intends to move *outside* of the country? In that case, all bets are off. If your infant is about to be taken outside of the country, you need to move fast to get your local court to step in and take action to slow down or stop the move.

This is a bad situation because once your co-parent leaves the country, you may have to find a lawyer in another country and navigate that country's laws to keep your parenting rights. If your co-parent is trying to take the child overseas, it is a clear signal they really don't value your relationship with your child, and you can bet they won't make it easy to be found. The rest of this book's information is a moot point if you allow the other parent to leave the country with your child, so don't waste a moment finding legal help if you think this is a possibility. Furthermore, this would be a clear sign you have a high-conflict situation on your hands, and you should seek further assistance from a professional who deals in this specialty.

The last thing to make sure of is that you hire a reputable family law lawyer who actually practices family law. One of Jessica and Bill's most significant problems during their custody battle was that Bill used his friend, an injury attorney, as his legal counsel. The guy passed the bar exam, but he did not practice family law. Bill got terrible advice on multiple instances and topics. He showed up to court hearings unprepared more than once. Jess and Bill are both very reasonable people, and now they get along great. But back then, Bill's expectations on what was reasonable were totally off base, thanks to his inexperienced attorney.

As a result, they had a much harder time coming to an agreement, and Jess spent a lot more money fighting through the system than she otherwise would have. Paying an attorney sucks, but it's usually smarter than not paying one. You need their expertise, but if you want to keep your bills down, you have to keep your questions concise, which you are learning to do by reading this book.

If your case is especially complicated or involves large child support payments, then you might want to pay up for an attorney who is a member of the American Academy of Matrimonial Lawyers (AAML). This organization contains only the cream of the crop. Membership is difficult to attain, the first requirement being at least ten years practicing law. There are only about 1,650 AAML-certified lawyers in the country at the time of this writing. You can read about their qualifications and search for AAML-certified lawyers at their website, AAML.org. To be sure, there are many high-quality non-AAML attorneys, but if you want to find *and pay for* one of the best, then this is where to look.

Custody — Physical vs. Legal and Sole vs. Joint

Once you determine the right jurisdiction and find your lawyer, the next thing to think about is what kind of custody arrangement you will seek. The terms can get a little confusing, but it's not that complicated.

The words "sole custody" means one parent has custody, while the term "joint custody" means both parents share custody approximately equally. Think of "joint custody" as nearly 50/50 and "sole custody" to something closer to 75/25.

Additionally, there is also "physical custody," which refers to who the child resides with, and "legal custody," which refers to who has legal decision-making authority. A co-parent can have either sole or joint *physical* custody and sole or joint *legal* custody.

Most (but not all) states differentiate between legal custody and physical custody, meaning they are two separate issues that need to be resolved individually. Alternatively, some states consider them to be connected, meaning they are a package deal. In these states, sole physical custody comes with sole legal custody attached to it, and joint physical custody comes with joint legal custody attached. Again, most states make a distinction such that you can have sole physical custody and joint legal custody, as was the case with Jessica and Bill in Pennsylvania, as well as Mary and me in Maryland.

If you have *sole* physical custody, it means the child lives with you and the other parent has visitation rights. If you have *joint* physical custody, it means the child splits his time nearly 50/50 between the two homes. Joint physical custody is possible only if the two homes are reasonably close geographically. Mrs. Big made it clear to me on day one that there was no way I would win joint physical custody in a trial if I lived in New York and Mary continued to live in Maryland. It just wasn't in the child's best interest to travel back and forth that sort of distance every few days. I could hardly argue with that, and I could not relocate due to my profession, so I had to settle for standard visitation rights rather than joint physical custody.

Joint physical custody with a 50/50 time split is most common in divorce cases where the parents will live nearby each other, and it can be argued the child is better off seeing each parent equally because that is what they are already used to. Older kids can definitely split their time 50/50 between two parents living in the same school district, but with infants, historically there has been a higher chance that one party (usually the mother) will have sole physical custody.

When infants are involved, sometimes the mother pushes hard for sole custody, and opinions vary widely on what age is right for children to spend large amounts of time away from her. Both Jess and Mary got sole physical custody, and Bill did not even live that far away from Jess at the time— less than an hour's drive. While the bar is higher for joint physical custody when infants are involved, we believe there is no reason a child older than one year cannot spend equal time with both parents, assuming they live near each other. Of course, if either parent has some sort of mental health or substance abuse problem, then all the expectations are thrown out the window.

Co-parents can agree to almost any arrangement that works for them. In some divorce cases, the children stay put in the same house, and each parent spends a few nights with the child and then moves out so the other parent can move in for a few nights. This sort of arrangement is unusual and probably not going to work for most of you.

If the parents cannot come to an agreement, the judge will eventually decide the physical custody issue. We believe when infants are concerned, judges *may* be more likely to award the mother sole physical custody and give the father frequent visitation rights rather than 50/50 joint physical custody. This is what both Jess and I were told ten years ago.

However, we think the trend in recent years is moving in favor of 50/50 physical custody, even with infants, unless there is a good reason to award sole physical custody. "Good reason" usually means a long geographic distance between parents, but there could be other factors, such as one parent not having a suitable location to care for the child.

You may hear the terms "2-2-3" or "2-2-5-5" which are shorthand for common 50/50 joint physical custody schedules. You want short visits with frequent transitions for the youngest kids, so they are not away from either parent for too long. In a seven-day week, 2-2-3 means two days with Mom, two days with Dad, and three days with Mom. Next week, the roles reverse so that Dad has two, Mom two, and Dad three. This schedule doesn't work unless you live nearby one another.

For older kids with 50/50 joint custody, you can do 2-2-5-5, which splits up fourteen days into two with Mom, two with Dad, five with Mom, five with Dad, and then it repeats. This schedule cuts down on the transitions and allows for some longer periods together.

Again, the above schedules apply only to 50/50 joint physical custody arrangements when the parties live nearby. It is difficult to say whether the trend is shifting to 50/50 shared time for infants. You will need to discuss this issue with your attorney, who will help you identify all the factors and point you to a custody solution that is legally realistic in your jurisdiction and best for your child.

If you are reading this and realizing you are unlikely to have 50/50 joint physical custody, do not despair. You will still have overnight, unsupervised visits with your child; it just won't be as frequently as half the days of the year. You are no less of a parent than your counterpart, and you are probably doing what's best for your child.

Parents who are hoping or asking for 50/50 joint physical custody only because they want to lower their child support obligation should rethink that strategy. We will discuss financial support at length in the next chapter, but suffice it to say, that is the wrong reason to push for joint physical custody.

If you find yourself in the all-too-common battle between mother asking for sole and father asking for joint physical custody of an infant, try going for a compromise. Offer joint physical custody but with a very long phase-in period whereby the infant spends more time with Mom in the early years, working up to 50/50 time with both parents as she approaches school age. The only problem with that would be if one party decided to move farther away, but you could deal with that in your agreement by writing that the party who moves will forfeit some time with the child or has to do all the long-distance traveling.

Regardless of your *physical* custody status, typically both parents should be able to get joint *legal* custody, which gives you 50/50 decision-making authority unless you are in one of those states that treat legal and physical custody as a package deal. Legal custody refers to the legal right to make important, long-term, life-altering decisions for your child. The two prominent examples would be health care and educational decisions. If your child develops a serious medical condition, for example, parents with joint legal custody would have an equal say in how it is handled. The same goes for educational decisions, such as which school to attend or whether the child should be held back a year.

Joint legal custody does not mean both parents can micromanage each other. The day-to-day decisions like bedtime, diet, screen time, etc., are not major life-changing decisions and are generally up to the parent who has the child that day to determine. However, it is advisable to get on the same page as your co-parent, when possible, so your child experiences consistency.

We believe there is a clear preference for most courts to award *joint* legal custody rather than *sole* legal custody unless one parent has abandoned the child or shown some other pattern of terribly poor decision-making. This is another issue you need local expertise on, so make sure to discuss your state's laws with your attorney. In our experience, poorly managed expectations of how the courts would rule on physical and legal custody were largely responsible for the prolonged legal battles between Mary and me and Jessica and Bill.

In Bill's case, at first, he was pushing for *sole* physical custody, which we can only imagine was based on bad advice from his attorney friend. Later, he reduced his ask to *joint* physical custody, but his lawyer still should have known he was unlikely to get joint physical custody in a trial. Jessica knew this and was happy to give Bill standard visitation rights but not 50/50 time. Therefore, they battled for a year before Bill realized he was asking for something unreasonable, thanks to his inexperienced attorney.

In Mary's case, her expectations about *legal* custody were unreasonable and partly responsible for our first legal battle. I conceded right away that she would have sole physical custody given our long distance, but I was not willing to give up my parental decision-making rights. I insisted on joint legal custody, and it was a deal breaker for me. Mrs. Big made it clear I should hold firm on joint legal custody because I was likely to get it in a trial, and she thought Mary's attorneys were probably advising her the same thing.

Still, Mary was just not willing to share decision-making power with me. As a result, we spent tens of thousands of dollars preparing for a trial only to come to a compromise just days before our trial. The compromise was that I would have joint legal custody, except Mary would have the final say concerning educational decisions. I still have a voice in educational decisions, but Mary has the final decision-making power if we cannot agree. I compromised on this point to avoid the trial and because I trusted that Mary would make decent educational decisions. Sometimes you have to ask yourself, what are you so afraid of? Giving in on this point was one of the things I did right in our battle.

Please take another look at the recap of the terms below. This is one of the most important things to learn in this book, so make sure you understand the differences between these types of custody and discuss with your attorney what your expectations should be in your circumstance.

Sole Physical Custody — The child resides with one parent most of the time, and the other parent has regular visitation rights. With infants, the courts were historically more likely to award mothers sole physical custody and give the father regular visitation rights, although there may be a trend toward joint physical custody in recent years. Mary has sole physical custody of Kelly, and Jessica has sole physical custody of Adam, while Bill and I have standard visitation rights.

Joint Physical Custody — The child spends approximately equal time residing with both parents. This works only when the homes are near each other geographically. It is typical in divorce cases with older children but probably becoming the default in most cases with younger children too. Most courts want both parents to be equally involved whenever possible.

Sole Legal Custody — One parent, the one with sole physical custody, has all the decision-making rights concerning major life-altering decisions for the child, such as health care and education. The parent with visiting rights can make minor day-to-day decisions independently, but they have no legal authority to make life-altering, long-term decisions for the child. This arrangement is unusual unless you are in a state where they lump legal and physical custody together or unless one parent has a history of abandonment or is somehow shown to be unfit to make decisions.

Joint Legal Custody — Both parents have equal legal decision-making rights concerning major, life-altering decisions such as health care and educational decisions. The courts want the child to benefit from both parents' input and, therefore, typically award joint legal custody unless there is a strong reason to limit one parent's authority or unless you are in one of those package deal states that lump legal and physical custody together. Both Bill and I have joint legal custody of our kids even though we are the visiting parents.

Visitation Rights

As with custody issues, if your expectations are in line with reality concerning visitation, then you should not have any reason to get in a legal battle with your co-parent. Unfortunately, visitation, especially when an infant is concerned, is often an emotional issue that can be very hard, especially for the mothers. For a good reason! Mothers carried the little person in their belly for nine months. Guys, make sure to cut Mom some slack if she has a hard time letting her newborn out of her sight.

As hard as it is, most new mothers understand Dad will sooner or later have unsupervised overnight visits at his home on a regular basis. But they are not sure at what age the courts will grant these visits. Moms instinctually want to protect their young and are often unwilling to part for even short periods. In some cases, they might be right to worry if the father has no history with children or no support network to help, such as the child's grandparents. Furthermore, if Mom is nursing, it can be a challenge to pump milk for the father to use during his visits, and shouldn't that count for something? Won't the court understand that it's just too soon for visits away from Mom?

On the other hand, fathers sometimes lash out and demand immediate private visitation as if they are not doing their fatherly duty if they don't have "alone time" visits from day one. They tend to want to spend time with their child on their turf, unsupervised by a mother and perhaps other maternal family members with whom they may not get along.

But, deep down, fathers know (or will soon learn) the truth: the first few months of an infant's life consist of nursing, pooping, and sleeping around the clock, so there is not really much reason to insist on overnight private visits at first. Yes, you want the newborn to learn your look, voice, smell, etc. However, you just don't need overnight or even private visits to achieve this during the first year. I know from experience that short but frequent visits will do the job. But still, how long will the court make you wait before you have some private time? She's your baby, too, right?

Even though everyone agrees a time will come when Dad gets unsupervised overnight visits, the problem is co-parents often cannot agree on *when* exactly this will happen.

Again, correctly managing your expectations will be the difference between an expensive court battle and a seamless transition. The first component to consider is simply the child's age. A newborn baby will not have unsupervised or overnight visits with their father in the first few months unless the mother wants it to happen. After all, it will take several months after the birth to get the first court hearing, so the earliest a father could even think about forcing overnight visits is somewhere around six months but probably closer to twelve months old.

At six months, infants can begin to sample solid foods. Although they will still rely heavily on breast milk or formula for nourishment, the argument that they *must* remain with their mother to nurse doesn't hold much water after six months of age. At least that's what Jess's attorney advised her the Pennsylvania judges would say, and it's what Mrs. Big believed would hold true in Maryland. Mary disagreed wholeheartedly; she felt that Kelly had to remain close by for years to continue nursing around the clock.

Mary was also deeply concerned about something known as "stranger anxiety." This is a clinical term used to describe how infants typically get nervous and cry around unfamiliar people. It does indeed happen, and it is a real thing. According to attachment parenting principles, stranger anxiety should be avoided at all costs because the theory preaches the worst thing you can do is let an infant cry.

However, according to most parents who have ever left a child with a babysitter or a grandparent for a few hours, stranger anxiety is nothing to worry about at all. The child will get used to the person and stop crying in short order, guar-an-teed. If you are really concerned about it, the best cure for stranger anxiety is to introduce the new person slowly in small doses, working up to longer exposures. It may take a few visits, but the child will be perfectly fine with the newcomer sooner or later. In the meantime, you can be sure there is no lasting damage done from crying a bit while Mom is away.

We don't mean to sound coldhearted, but every infant cries at times, and it is perfectly natural. After all, they can't talk! Crying is their only way to communicate, and you shouldn't ignore it. Of course, you must check to see their diaper is dry, their belly is full, a clothing tag is not irritating them, etc. But you don't need to worry they will harm themselves by crying. Books like *Eat, Sleep, Poop* devote chapters to this sort of thing.

Our point is not how to best care for an infant. Our point is to make sure you understand the courts are not likely to take "stranger anxiety" as an excuse to withhold unsupervised visits. The cure for stranger anxiety is *more* time alone with the stranger, not less.

Despite Mary's fears, most parents and most courts believe there is no real reason a child cannot spend alone time, even overnight, away from its mother after six to nine months of age. This includes nursing babies.

The exception would be if the child has not seen the father very often, then Mom can make the case that a short "phase-in" period should be observed to mitigate the stranger anxiety before the first extended overnight visits. No one wants to drop off a baby for a weekend with someone the baby doesn't know at all. If Dad is smart, he should want to start with short visits and work up to longer ones. It will be easier for him as well as the child. Generally, the court will phase-in the father's alone time if the child doesn't know him already by ruling that the mother supervises the first three or four visits so the child can get used to Dad while Mom is still nearby.

Going weeks or months without seeing their child is a common mistake fathers make during custody battles, although sometimes it is out of their control if the mother will not allow them to visit. Bill made this mistake during his custody battle with Jessica. Although Jessica was willing to allow supervised visits with Adam from day one, Bill was wrapped up in the legal fight and felt unwelcome at Jessica's home to boot. He was not willing to visit Adam on Jessica's terms, and as a result, almost a year went by before the custody battle was over and Bill began regular visits. Because Adam had not seen his father much during that first year, Bill had to agree to a phasing-in period of four short, supervised visits before longer unsupervised visits began. Again, if Bill had had a *family* law attorney, he probably would have been advised to handle this differently.

Mrs. Big made it clear to me from the beginning that the best thing I could do, both as a parent and as a litigant asking the court to grant visitation rights, was to make sure I saw my child as often as possible on whatever terms Mary would allow. Mary was happy to have me visit Kelly as often as I liked but only in her home while she was nearby. I followed my attorney's advice, and for every single weekend from birth till age one, I visited my daughter in Maryland. I did not have any unsupervised time until the courts required it about half-way through the battle, but those were just a few hours at a time and not yet overnight visits. This will make more sense in the next section when we spell out the timeline you should expect in a custody battle.

Aside from the legal custody (decision-making rights) dispute, overnight visitation was the other main issue that had Mary and me locked in litigation. During the pregnancy and after the birth, she made it clear she would not allow overnight visits in my home until Kelly was *four or five years old*. As the custody battle raged on, she lowered her age demand to two or three years old, but that was still too long for me. Mrs. Big assured me the courts would rule there was no reason to wait past age one year, which coincided with our trial date.

As I mentioned earlier, Mary had gone all-in on the attachment parenting beliefs, and she was scared to death that any separation from her would traumatize our child. "Traumatizing" is a word she often used to describe what she thought visits with me would be like for Kelly. I believe she had been feeling some sort of attachment parenting guilt, which we assume is common with new mothers who sub-scribe to attachment parenting. They want to be the "best mother ever," and everything outside of their control becomes a threat to that impossible ideal.

It seemed to me that Mary felt she had to protect Kelly from visits with me because she feared it might do mental or physical damage or somehow weaken their mother-child bond. Of course, I disagreed, and I wanted to start making my own bond with Kelly. But more importantly, the courts disagree, and because Mary was unwilling to align her expectations about visitation and legal custody with reality, we began a long and expensive court battle when Kelly was about one month old.

Our custody battle took almost a year to play out, which is typical. In the end, we settled without a trial, but part of our settlement was that I had to agree to an additional twelve-month phase-in period. Meaning, I had to slowly phase-in regular weekend overnight visits for *another* twelve months even though I had spent the *previous* twelve months visiting Kelly in Maryland every single weekend. Why would I agree to such a thing if Mrs. Big told me the courts would grant immediate overnight visits? My thinking will make more sense as we move through the next few sections.

Custody Litigation Timeline

This was a shock to us. Some jurisdictions move faster than others, but if this is your first experience with litigation, the process will likely move slower than you thought it would. In most jurisdictions, a custody battle is expected to take at least a year from when one party files the initial custody complaint to the day of your trial (assuming you do not settle your case sometime before that). This long, drawn-out process is partly because, in most jurisdictions, there just are not enough resources to get through the massive backlog of cases any faster.

However, the slow timeline is also partly by design. The court system desperately wants you to settle your custody battle without ever going to trial. Ask anyone who has experience with the system—attorneys, judges, other parents—and they will all tell you the same thing, which is, "The last person you want deciding your custody agreement is a judge."

This is perhaps the most important thing you can learn from this book, certainly from this chapter. No judge cares about you and your unique family situation as much as you and your child's co-parent do. No judge will ever be able to craft a proper parenting plan that is as detailed as you want. No judge will agree with your entire point of view, no matter how right your position is. And no judge will be able to solve the ongoing problems you are sure to encounter in the years to come.

Hence, the drawn-out litigation timeline almost feels like someone designed it to test your patience. It slow-walks you through one step after another, with weeks or months in between steps, down the long road to the worst-case outcome, which is an expensive, stressful trial where no one really wins. At every stop on the path to trial, the system attempts to push you closer to a legal settlement. A settlement means coming to an agreement with your co-parent before going to trial, and it is almost always preferable to a trial.

Settlement can be confusing to people. I think Mary at first thought that getting the law involved would automatically lead to a scary courtroom trial situation like you see on TV. Just the opposite is true, which I confess I, too, did not understand at first. At least not until I paid Mrs. Big to explain it to me.

It works like this. One parent initiates the court process because they want to formalize the custody, visitation, and child support payments. The other parent either agrees to the terms the first parent proposed or not. Even if you both agree on everything, you still need to go through the legal channels to formalize the agreement.

You might think, why bother going through the formal legal system if we agree on everything? Remember, just because you get along well now doesn't mean you will for the next eighteen years. And, no matter what, your child deserves to have both parents legally recognized, so it is important you get this taken care of the right way.

If there is agreement on the issues, the attorneys draft what's called a "parenting plan" and submit it to the courts for approval (more on parenting plans later). As long as the agreement fits within the judge's definition of "reasonable," then he will stamp the plan with his approval, and the co-parents go on their merry way, avoiding a costly and lengthy legal battle.

However, if there is not agreement on all the issues, and there is usually not, then you will start down the long and expensive road to a trial where eventually a judge will hear both sides and decide on custody, visitation, and child support. The problem is, by the time you get to a trial, you will have spent a fortune in legal bills, you will be stressed out beyond belief, and in the end, the judge will not give you the results you wanted.

Even if you "win" your trial by getting the custody or visitation you asked for, there will not be the level of detail you hoped for in the ruling. You will continue arguing with your co-parent over little things like "Where do we meet?" and "What about holidays?" and other such issues the judge did not address but that come up in life frequently. There is no jury in these cases, so your fate hinges on the whims of one person who has heard it all before and very likely does not think your big issues are nearly as important as you do. Hopefully, the judge isn't feeling cranky for any reason on the day of your trial.

So, if you really want to save money *and* months of anxiety *and* get a better outcome, then have your co-parent read this book and learn the meaning of the word *compromise*. If you each compromise early in the process, then you can wrap up everything without paying your lawyers for more than a few hours of drafting and filing paperwork with the court.

There was a time early in the pregnancy when I thought this would happen for Mary and me, but then I realized she didn't want me to have joint legal custody or overnight visitation for several years. Since I had decided those were deal-breaker issues for me, we marched on down the path to trial. Similarly, Jess and Bill went through months of litigation because Bill started out unreasonably asking for sole physical custody, an outcome he had no business asking for.

If your attorneys are good at their jobs, they should encourage both of you to ask only for what is reasonable. They should constantly be nudging you to compromise and take steps toward settlement, as Mrs. Big did with me. If you find yourself with an attorney who is pushing you to trial, then you should be questioning whether they are more interested in what's best for you or what will lead to the most billable hours for them.

Perhaps a list is the clearest way to show what you should expect. Although each state will have its own legal timeline and terminology, they all share common steps. Your lawyer can help you with the details in your jurisdiction, but here are the steps in generalized terms that you should expect to go through:

1. During the pregnancy, find a lawyer and do some background research to make sure you understand the basics about custody laws in the state that applies to your situation. Encourage your co-parent to read this book!

2. Get through the birth. Focus on the baby and mother's recovery for at least a few weeks. Legal actions don't need to start right away, but it is a long process, so don't wait too long either.

3. Sometime in the first few months of the child's life, have a serious heart to heart with your co-parent about custody issues. Tell your co-parent you want to get the custody and child support payments formalized for the child's sake and you don't think there is any reason there needs to be a legal battle of any kind. Tell your co-parent you want to pay (or receive) the standard child support amounts calculated by the state (no more, no less). Hopefully, if both parties are reasonable and mature, this conversation ends with something like, "Okay, I'll tell my lawyer to call your lawyer, and they can work out the details."

4. Get the legal ball rolling in the first few months of the child's life, right after your heart-to-heart talk. Child support payments do not start to accrue until one party files the initial paperwork with the courts, so if you are on the receiving end, you will want to start that clock. But another reason is you just don't want years to go by before deciding to ask the court for parenting rights. Waiting that long begs the question, "Why did you wait so long to protect your rights?"

5. The legal process starts when one party's attorney draws up the legal petition for custody and files it with the court. Assuming you are not yet in full agreement with your co-parent on custody terms, the paperwork that gets filed is simply a document that says, "My client wants joint legal custody, standard visitation rights, and standard child support," or whatever you and your lawyer decide is reasonable to ask for.

6. The court approves and returns your petition a few weeks later, but it is not yet active until you officially serve the

document to your co-parent. To "serve" someone a legal document typically means someone other than the party filing the complaint (someone other than you) must physically hand the envelope with the petition in it to the defendant (your co-parent) and then sign an affidavit stating that they have done so at this time and place. It is usually acceptable to serve the documents to your co-parent's attorney if they are willing to accept them. If you are on the receiving end of a legal petition, don't try to run or hide from the documents. Someone will find and serve you eventually, and anything you do to disrupt the legal process will just make you look bad in the eyes of the law.

7. Once the petition for custody has been served, the clock starts ticking toward a trial, and child support payments begin to accrue, meaning the paying parent will owe support as of this date. From here on, each state can vary in how they do things. Still, it is safe to assume there will be at least two or three court hearings (appearances), each several months apart, before you get a trial date that is probably about a year after you first served your co-parent the legal complaint.

8. One of the first hearings you will attend is designed to take care of any pressing problems that cannot wait for trial. In Maryland, it was called a "pendente lite hearing," and it usually took place three or four months after the initial filing of the custody complaint. For example, at this hearing, the court might insist on at least limited visitation if one parent did not allow the other to see the child at all. It might also insist on some minimum amount of child support payments to begin if there is clearly going to be support required later. The point of this first hearing is to make sure neither party is being blatantly wronged

or damaged by the other and by the long wait for trial. During this pendente lite hearing, the court insisted Mary start to allow me to see Kelly for several hours unsupervised during my weekend visits to Maryland.

9. Forced mediation sessions with a neutral third party trained to help you settle your case will likely be part of the court's required steps to complete sometime before a trial. You typically do these without your attorney present. These sessions can actually be very beneficial. You should take them seriously and perhaps even push for more mediation time than the minimum required by the court if you find you are making progress. Mediators also charge by the hour but typically less than your lawyer, and you will get much more bang for your buck sitting with a mediator for an hour than with your lawyers.

10. There will be a couple of months dedicated to "discovery," which starts about halfway through the process when each party asks the other for just about every piece of information that might be useful in the litigation. The keyword is "might" because 95% of it is useless, but the lawyers must ask for everything to be thorough. We will discuss the discovery phase in more detail in the next section. For now, just understand you will need to answer written questions called interrogatories and supply box after box of financial statements and other personal documents. If you have not settled your case by the discovery phase of the litigation, then you better have some cash on hand because this is where the legal bills start to grow exponentially.

11. There are other steps the legal process will require, all designed to push you to a settlement without trial. In

Maryland, I recall one of the hearings we had to attend was presided over by a retired family law judge. He listened to our lawyers state our differences, and then he gave us a twenty-minute lecture about how our child's very life depends on us getting along better. He told a long-winded but heartfelt story about the co-parents of a teenager who refused to communicate and work together. The teenager told each parent that she was staying with the other parent one night, when in fact, she was sneaking out with her friends and getting into trouble. Because the parents refused to work together, they didn't realize the danger their daughter was in, and tragically she died that night in some terrible way that could have been prevented if the parents had simply touched base with each other.

12. There will likely be online classes the court requires you to complete. I remember several online courses I had to take about healthy co-parenting and childcare, all with various deadlines for completion before the trial. I also recall being forced to watch a video produced by the Maryland legal system that emphasized how terrible going to trial would be. It showed how the notion that many people have about "getting your day in court" is just not realistic.

Like many people frustrated by a co-parent or the legal system, I had this fantasy daydream of taking the witness stand and blowing the judge's socks off with my extraordinary evidence and tales of unbelievable injustice I had endured. I imagined I could eloquently and passionately explain how wrong Mary was all these months, and if I could just get him to listen to reason, then he would surely rule in my favor. And, of course, I figured Mary would look like a fool when Mrs. Big exposed all the terrible positions she held. Part of me looked forward to my day in court when "she would get what was coming to her." Wrong!

This video everyone had to watch made the point that your day in court is likely to go nothing like your daydream fantasy. In reality, you will spend a fortune on trial preparation. On the day of the trial, most of that preparation won't even get used, but the bills will keep racking up as the hours tick by. On the witness stand, you will likely freeze up and not tell your story as well as you thought you would in your daydreams. On cross-examination, the opposing attorney will probably embarrass you or make you out to be something you're not. In the end, the judge will figure both of you are bending the truth a bit, and he will not side entirely with either of you. You will end up with a vague ruling that does not solve all your problems but instead leaves you feeling unsatisfied, still angry, and with much less money than you had the day before. The video drove home the message, "Settle your case! Avoid a trial at all costs."

13. If the months keep ticking by without a settlement, you will eventually get to something called a settlement hearing or a pre-trial hearing. This is the court's last attempt to push you to settle without a trial. The attorneys will explain where the differences are to the court. The judge will tell the attorneys to push for compromise one last time. In the next few weeks, you will have a trial if you don't come to an agreement.

14. With the trial date fast approaching, your lawyer will now start working around the clock on "trial prep." Mrs. Big explained that it's better to delay trial prep as long as possible because you don't want to pay your attorney for all that work if you end up settling a few weeks before

the trial. Trial prep includes gathering up and organizing all the documents and evidence you will need, formulating arguments and lines of questioning for each witness, and anticipating what your opponent will attack you with. It's a lot of work and stress once you realize the big day is right around the corner now. People often come to their senses at this point when they realize they don't want to answer personal questions in a courtroom and that maybe all those people who said to avoid a trial were right.

15. Trial day—sometimes multiple days. We have never actually sat through a trial, so we will not pretend to be an expert on this. All we know is that you will almost certainly be better off settling than with a trial. I avoided one in part by having a heart-to-heart with Mary about a week before our trial date. I told her what she already knew from months of our negotiations, that I would be willing to do a long phase-in to overnight visits but I would not wait for years, and I had to have joint legal custody. I also told her in clear terms that if we went to trial next week, I would be asking for immediate overnight visits. I think she knew I would get them because her lawyer was as good as mine and certainly told her as much.

   We ended up writing a parenting plan in the thirty-six hours before our trial and hashed out the final tweaks on the courtroom steps, literally. I remember entering the courtroom with the settlement in hand (you have to submit your agreement to the judge for him to dismiss your case) and being so thankful that the stress of the trial was now gone. A courtroom is a nerve-racking place by design. We repeat: avoid a trial at all costs.

Evidence in a Custody Case

You may be thinking, *Evidence? This isn't a crime scene. Evidence of what?* There are at least three major reasons you will need to gather and supply evidence during the discovery phase of your litigation: child support calculations, legal custody decisions, and visitation rights.

For starters, the courts will have to do a calculation to figure out who owes who child support and how much. We will get into the calculation more in the next chapter, but both parties will need to turn over all their financial records, and attorneys will want to see all kinds of documents to make sure no one is hiding income to tilt the calculation in their favor. This can be especially important when one party owns a small business or gets paid under the table in cash or other unconventional means.

Another need for evidence will be if one party is contesting joint legal custody. If one party is making the claim that the other parent should not have decision-making rights, they will need to show the courts some justification for this request. If you ask for sole legal custody, the implication is your child would be better off without the other parent's input in crucial life decisions, either because of their long history of poor judgment or for some other reason.

In my case, Mary tried to argue that we did not see eye to eye on anything, and therefore Kelly would be better off without my parenting input. Thus, Mary's attorney was looking for evidence that showed we just couldn't get along in the past. Mrs. Big believed Mary's argument was weak and wouldn't persuade the judge to take away my parenting rights. However, we still looked for examples of decisions Mary and I had successfully made together to counterbalance Mary's points.

Visitation is the third major area where evidence comes into play. In my case, there was powerful evidence in favor of immediate overnight visits because I had seen my daughter every single weekend of her life. Most of my recent visits were unsupervised once the court insisted on it at the pendente lite hearing when Kelly was about six months old. On the other side, Mary was trying to show evidence that Kelly would have stranger anxiety if she were away from her mother for any length of time by claiming that our infant cried occasionally. She also argued my visits would interrupt breast-feeding, which, of course, didn't hold much weight as Kelly approached age one.

Mary's arguments against overnight visitation—stranger anxiety and nursing past one year—were almost silly, and everyone involved in my case knew it, including my lawyer, her lawyers, our various mediators, and anyone else you asked. But there can be legitimate reasons to protest unsupervised or overnight visits, including substance abuse, domestic violence, or mental illness. Each of those are serious accusations, and you should not even think of making them unless you have genuine evidence to back up your concerns.

You should also know there are rules about evidence that lawyers follow. Without getting too in the weeds here, the evidence has to be unaltered, taken in context (rather than taken out of context), and shared in advance during the discovery phase. For example, if you want to show a nasty text message that someone sent you, you cannot just present a few rows of offensive words by themselves. You cannot alter or highlight parts to make them stand out. You have to share the entire history of all text messages between the two parties in advance during the discovery phase. It must include everything relevant to the situation, not just the nasty lines you want the judge to read.

For example, your attorney can present in trial something like, "On page fifty-six of your text messages with my client, there is a text that says XYZ . . ." But the opposing attorney must have the chance to cross-examine with something like, "Yes, but on page thirty-two, you sent a contradictory text that says ZYX . . ." The judge must be able to read the full context of the larger conversation. Everything must be shared with the opposing attorney in advance; otherwise, it will likely be inadmissible in your trial.

Now, is it likely the judge will be influenced by the nonsense the two of you texted or emailed back and forth to each other all year? Probably not, especially if it is just emotional garbage. But be advised that all emails, texts, photos, and voicemails will be fair game. So if your co-parent is trying to paint you as a drunk, you probably don't want to text about the weekend bender you were just on while the other parent was watching the child. You don't want to give the other parent any material that could be potentially harmful in a trial. Best to keep your messages polite, cordial, and informational based. No sarcasm. No swear words. Keep it clean, and no one can accuse you of being otherwise.

Your lawyer will guide you on evidence rules, so there is not too much for you to worry about here, except for one crucial thing. Video and audio recordings have special rules that vary from state to state. Some states allow for hidden recordings, meaning recordings are permitted without the person's expressed consent, and other states do not. If you are in a state that requires consent, do not, under any circumstances, make an audio or video recording without getting consent on the recording from the person you are recording. Not only will the evidence be thrown out of your custody trial but you will also be inviting a serious criminal or civil lawsuit. Check with Google and your attorney to be sure what the rules are in your state.

We were quite surprised at the amount of work involved during the discovery phase of our custody battles. Our attorneys had their junior (cheaper) associates do a lot of the legwork, but regardless, the hours involved for both you and your attorney are just staggering. After all, your lawyer can only prepare the evidence you provide her. She cannot gather your bank statements and answer long personal questions without input from you. The discovery process will cost you not only money but also many, many hours of your life. It begins about four to six months after your lawsuit begins. Here is what exactly to expect.

First, you are likely to get a long list of "interrogatories," which are pointed questions you must reply to in writing under oath. Well, actually, you must pay your lawyer to type up your answers in an official response that gets filed with the court. Two examples of interrogatories I received from Mary's attorneys were:

> List and itemize any and all additional financial benefits that you receive from your employment, including but not limited to rental reimbursements, travel expenses, entertainment expenses reimbursements, use of a company car, reimbursement for the use of your own motor vehicle, and state the amount of such benefits that you have received from your employer during the past twelve months.

> Describe in detail the nature of any and all disagreements which you and the Defendant have, or have had, concerning your daughter, including but not limited to previous visitation, the child's religion or religious upbringing, future daycare, health care, education, living arrangements or other matters on which you have not been able to agree.

Second, discovery also includes "document requests" in which you are asked to turn over every monthly financial statement going back about three years, including invest-ments, checking accounts, credit cards, paychecks, tax returns, and even applications for loans. Every email and text message between you and your co-parent must be disclosed whether you think it's relevant or not. Your personal calendar and jour-nal, any receipts or photos that matter, and of course, you must hand over any data collected from co-parenting apps like Our Family Wizard, which is a tool we will discuss later. It can be boxes and boxes full of documents if you have to print them, which you typically do. And then you pay your lawyer to look through all the documents from you and from your co-parent, which amounts to many hours of billable work.

I can remember dutifully producing and categorizing every document Mary's attorney asked for. It was all there and well-or-ganized in folders too. I believe the only document they asked for but I couldn't produce (because I didn't have it anymore) was the insensitive talking points I brought with me to dinner that night during the pregnancy. But Mary's side didn't produce a number of the documents we asked for, and it was only near the trial date that I realized you cannot force someone to produce a document they don't want to produce. They will say it's lost or unavailable or some other excuse for it not being there. The trial will go on, and the judge might shake his head in disgust and maybe slap them on the wrist, but if it's not there, then it's not there. A critical missing document, like a tax return, might cause serious repercussions, but a minor missing document, like a specific email, won't stop the trial from proceeding.

Third, in some cases, there will be "depositions," which are in-person interviews where you get grilled under oath by the opposing attorney during the discovery phase, months before the trial. Your answers are recorded (perhaps even on video), and the interview can literally go on for as long as the attorney wants to take it. You can be sure the transcript of everything you say will be combed over and used against you in the trial if they can show you contradicted yourself in any way. Again, your attorney will rack up many billable hours to prepare for the deposition, actually sit through it (both in your defense and when deposing your co-parent), and afterward to analyze the transcripts.

In my case, Mrs. Big deposed Mary because we wanted her to admit for the record that she really believed some of her more outlandish positions, including those on attachment parenting, stranger anxiety, breastfeeding well past infancy, and her objections to overnight visits. On the other hand, Mary's attorney did not bother deposing me—I can only imagine because he felt it would be a waste of time and money since I was not asking for anything out of the ordinary.

Finally, in some cases where people really want to throw their money away, there will be so-called "expert witnesses" called into play. This happens when, for example, one parent hires a child psychologist or physician to testify about some specific concern. To be a credible witness, they have to spend many hours with the child, and they often charge as much or more per hour than attorneys do. The standard legal response to one party introducing an expert witness is simply hiring an opposing "expert," paying them to spend the same number of hours with the child, and testifying to the complete opposite point of view. Thankfully, we avoided this charade because our children had no special needs, and our lawyers told us that any "experts" generally cancel each other out in the trial and so they are just not worth the money unless you have an extraordinary situation.

What Is a Parenting Plan?

We have mentioned a parenting plan a few times now, and you may be wondering what exactly it means. A personalized parenting plan is the goal of your custody battle. It's the holy grail you seek. It is elusive and rare to find early in the process, but if you are lucky, mature, and willing to compromise, then there is no reason you cannot agree on a plan even before you begin your custody battle or a few months into it at the worst.

When we use the words "parenting plan," we are referring to a settlement agreement, written and signed by both co-parents, that spells out the parties' rights and obligations regarding each other and their child. It is a document that describes financial child support obligations, legal custody, and visitation rights. It is a product of both parties compromising and respecting each other's roles. It will contain some standard legal language, but it will be customized to suit your child's unique situation.

If you are stubborn, unreasonable, misinformed, vindictive, or trying to block the other parent's rights, then you are unlikely to agree on a parenting plan unless one side is just so afraid of legal confrontation that they fold without a fight. Barring that exception, without a compromise, you will end up in a custody trial where the judge will pull out a standardized document and write in your names and a few minor changes before stamping it and sending you on your way. His "off the shelf" parenting plan will not work very well for either of you or your child.

But if you can find the wisdom and patience to compromise, you will have a much better parenting plan, customized to your unique situation. The customized parenting plan will be drafted by your attorneys, undergoing several iterations as it passes back and forth between the two parties. Each attorney will make sure their client's most important needs and wishes are addressed while encouraging them to loosen up on the points that just aren't worth fighting over in the long run.

Eventually, if you have a signed agreement before your trial, it will be submitted to the court as part of a filing known as a "consent order." A consent order announces to the court that you have settled your differences and you both agree to terminate your litigation and live by the terms outlined in the document. The judge will approve nearly any agreement you come to with your co-parent so long as the basics are covered (financial support, legal custody, visitation) and as long as there is nothing in it that sounds nonsensical, harmful to the child, or likely to lead you back to court in short order.

At the end of this chapter, you will find a copy of the actual parenting plan written years ago between Mary and me, complete with the many flaws it contained. As you read through it, you will see our comments pointing out all the parts that worked well and the other parts I wish had been written differently, knowing what I know now. It begins with a legally formatted consent order, followed by personalized parenting plan provisions. Your attorneys will draw up your consent order using the appropriate template and formatting for your legal jurisdiction; therefore, it won't look exactly like mine, but it will be similar in function.

You will see the consent order started by establishing I was our child's biological father born on X date. It states that we agree to share joint legal custody (Mary eventually gave in on this). It says that Mary had primary physical custody, and I would have visitation rights to be further outlined in detail in the "custody provisions" section of the document. Finally, it lays out child support payments amounting to $X and other financial issues concerning health insurance and legal bills, which we will discuss further in the next chapter.

The "custody provisions" referred to in the consent order is the part that is customizable to your specific situation and where you will do most of your compromising over minor issues such as holidays. If you work well with your co-parent, and you have a history of solving disagreements together, you might opt for a more generalized document that says things like "We will share holidays equally."

However, if you don't work well together and you are a stickler for details, then you will probably feel better with a document that tries to address every individual situation, such as "We define Christmas as forty-eight hours from noon December 24th to noon December 26th and will alternate that holiday each year."

If you are in a high-conflict situation, the professionals (like Brook Olsen at HighConflict.net) recommend making your document as detailed as you can to avoid future debates. While it's impossible to address every conceivable future contingency, Jess and I agree more detail is better than less. After all, if you are getting along great down the road, you can always toss the document aside and be flexible. But if you are prone to arguments, then a detailed plan is better than a vague one. If you are locked in a high-conflict battle with someone who will torment you at every turn, you will need a detailed document to show the authorities you were just following the agreement as it is written.

Mary and I had a parenting plan with custody provisions that were detailed, but in hindsight, not detailed enough. We started our document with about three pages of bullet points that one of the attorneys had pulled out of their desk drawer. They were all items that made sense to us, and they seemed like a good way to get some consensus going before we got to the more challenging subjects, such as vacation schedules. The list included things like "Neither parent will criticize or demean the other or the other's family either in or out of the child's presence," and "Each parent will respect time schedules and be prompt; when not possible notice shall be given as soon as possible to alert the other as to lateness and the reason." Many of these sounded needless to me. Obviously, we would tell each other if we were running late for a meeting, right? But we included them anyway.

The list of bullet points also had a few paragraphs concerning "dispute resolution," which we altered significantly after negotiating back and forth on this topic extensively. Dispute resolution concerns the steps we agreed to take to solve future disagreements using mediators or other methods rather than the court system. We will dig into this topic in the next section because dispute resolution is one of the most critical parts of your parenting plan and one of the most challenging parts to write efficiently.

After the three pages of bullet points on how we agreed to treat each other, you will see that our parenting plan had a long section spelling out my visitation access schedule. First, it described the twelve-month "phase-in" process, which I mentioned earlier. Phase one gave me longer and longer daytime visits for three months after we signed our agreement. Phase two lasted for six months after that and included single overnight stays every other weekend but only at my parents' home. Phase three lasted for three more months, now allowing full weekend overnight visits but again only in my parents' home. The phase-in would be complete after twelve months (Kelly's age two), at which point I would have my daughter every other weekend with no more geographic restrictions.

This extremely lengthy, twelve-month, drawn-out phase-in was unheard of and unnecessary from my perspective and everyone else involved in the case except Mary. But it was the only way I could get her to settle our litigation. Overnight visits petrified her, and I realized the only way they were going to happen would be either a judge forcing it in a trial or me agreeing to a ridiculously long phase-in as part of a settlement. I opted to avoid the trial. Besides, at this point, I wasn't entirely sure how well Kelly would do without her mom nearby since they were still nursing and co-sleeping in the same bed every day.

The permanent access schedule was described next in our parenting plan, as you will see below. It began at age twenty-four months and stated I would have forty-six-hour visits with Kelly every other weekend at the place of my choosing. Importantly, it said Mary and I would "share all the long-distance traveling burden equally up to a limit of the distance from Washington, DC to New York," and that "any distance beyond that was the responsibility of the party wishing to travel further away during their time with the child." This language would prove essential because transitions would be one of the issues we argued about repeatedly over the years to come.

I wanted to see Kelly more than every other weekend, but given the long distance, it seemed silly to write in something like "dinner every Wednesday night with father," which can work only when parents live closer together. We ended up including a vague provision that I could see Kelly for a few hours once a month on my "off" weekend in her hometown in Maryland. I tried to use this "right" for a few years, but Mary and I always had trouble agreeing on an exact time that worked for both of us, and these visits have become infrequent as Kelly got older and had various commitments on the weekends. But they did help me in the early years when more frequent interactions are important for building a relationship with a child. Nowadays, if there is a recital or big game or some reason for me to do an extra visit to Maryland, I do it. Mary usually cooperates because she knows Kelly wants me there and because we have yet another provision in our agreement that states I can attend all games, performances, recitals, and other activities as often as I like.

Holidays are described next in our custody provisions document. We didn't do a great job designing a holiday schedule, as you will see at the end of this chapter. It can be trickier than you think because some holidays are fixed— Martin Luther King Day is always the third Monday in January, while others float, like July 4th and Christmas. Typically, you alternate holidays from year to year. But what if Dad's MLK Monday holiday falls adjacent to Mom's weekend? You don't want your child to spend all weekend with Mom and then Monday with Dad; you want to keep the long holiday weekend intact. Otherwise, the holiday loses its value.

We tried to share all the major national holidays: Christmas, New Year's Day, MLK, Presidents' Day, Memorial Day, July 4th, Labor Day, and Thanksgiving. Some people also include Columbus Day or other less well-known days like "teacher in-service days," but we didn't. I wish now that I had included all school holidays like teacher in-service days in my negotiations, but at that point, the school years felt like a lifetime away. Besides, the lawyers kept saying we would probably have to revise the whole document when Kelly started school.

Mary also wanted language ensuring she was with Kelly on Mother's Day and Easter Sunday, so in return, I got Father's Day and Good Friday every year. We attempted to split Thanksgiving and Christmas into two blocks of time to be alternated each year. Our entire holiday section is quite poorly written, created many arguments, and didn't serve us well. We will give you some ideas for improving on my mistakes as you read through it.

Our summer vacation language was even more confusing than our holiday schedule and led to even more disputes in future years. Again, Mary insisted on a bit of a phasing-in. We started the first summer with a total of seven extra vacation days in addition to my regular alternating weekends, and each year it increased until reaching fourteen days by age four. Mary was torn between giving me Kelly for long stretches of consecutive days or lots of shorter visits peppered throughout the summer.

Importantly, our summer vacation language stated I would notify Mary of my chosen summer vacation days by April 1st each year and it was my unilateral choice as to which days I picked for vacation. Mary signed the document but reneged on that clause every year, claiming she ought to have a say in *when* exactly I take my vacation days. As a result, we had significant disputes each springtime concerning the upcoming summer.

Thinking back over the past decade, I'd have to say that holidays, summer vacation days, and even regular pickups/drop-offs for visit transitions created the most serious disputes between Mary and me. The disputes went on for years, led to litigation several years in a row, and are still a problem for us more than ten years later. So think carefully about these issues, but more importantly, think carefully about how you will resolve all the disputes that will arise in the future.

Dispute Resolution

The basic idea of dispute resolution provisions in a parenting plan is to lay out the steps you will follow in the event of a future parenting disagreement. The aim is to avoid going back to the court system when disputes inevitably arise.

You will see in our parenting plan shown below that our dispute resolution language started by stating we agreed to "Joint Legal Custody" and that "The parent with whom the child is at any time residing will have day-to-day parental responsibility, and each will respect the other's judgment... however, all decisions that have a significant, long-term impact on the child (education, health care, etc.) will be made by consensus unless in an emergency situation when the other parent is not able to be reached."

It went on to say, "Neither party shall act unilaterally to disturb the child's status quo . . . in the area of the child's health, education, religion, or wellbeing . . . in the event of disagreement, the following steps would be taken . . ."

The steps we agreed to were to "clearly identify the issue of disagreement" and then "use good faith to persuade each other" of our respective positions. If there was still disagreement, then we were to "identify an expert in the field of disagreement to assist us" in the dispute. If the difference persisted, we agreed to next "consult an individual known to both of us whom we trust to act as a mediator,"; failing that, we were to "employ a professional mediator" to help us reach a decision. Importantly, the professional mediator in this last step had no binding authority to force us to compromise.

Lastly, we agreed that if all the other steps were completed in good faith, then Mary would have the final say in all disputes concerning education decisions. It specified she would *not* have the final say for those disputes concerning the visitation schedule (transportation, meeting places, holidays, vacations, etc.), any decision that would commit me to expenses beyond those already spelled out, and any major medical decisions.

If those dispute resolution steps sound crazy and impractical to you, you would be right. They came about because Mary was contesting joint legal custody, and the only way she would allow me to have it is if I gave her the final say in disputes. But I wasn't willing to give her final say in *all* disputes, which would amount to effective sole legal custody. After many rounds of back and forth, we ended up with that long list of toothless steps, and I gave her the final say on educational decisions but not my visitation schedule, money issues, or medical decisions. Well, guess what almost all our disagreements have been about over the years? Yup, you guessed it: visitation schedules, money issues, and medical decisions (vaccines, etc.).

Compromise is how you avoid a trial. But compromise can also result in silly paragraphs like the dispute resolution steps Mary and I came up with. For starters, the steps took way too long. Many disputes need near-term resolutions because you don't tend to argue about things that are in the distant future. You typically argue about things that are happening this month, like what to do when there is snow in the forecast and one parent wants to cancel or postpone the weekend visit while the other does not. If your steps cannot handle near-term problems, then they won't be very useful.

Furthermore, our steps did not work well when Mary didn't want to engage in the process, which always seemed to be the case from my point of view. People say, "Possession is nine-tenths of the law," and this holds true in custody situations. For example, for several years, we argued about the Christmas holiday. I interpreted our document one way while she read it the other way. I remember this was a problem for us the first Christmas after settling our first case in September. We didn't even realize we had a dispute till the middle of December, so that didn't leave much time to go through the steps in our parenting plan.

I tried to start the dispute steps in writing, and Mary didn't even acknowledge my email for days. When I tried to push from step two to three to four, she said it wasn't possible to get through them all, given her busy schedule. She was happy with how things were (i.e., her interpretation of the holiday schedule). She had no motivation to quickly attend a mediation session with me to solve this amicably. Even if she had participated in mediation, the mediator would have had no power to force us to compromise. As a result, she got her way that Christmas because possession is nine-tenths of the law, leaving me with nothing but resentment and the realization that our dispute steps were virtually worthless.

When we wrote our original parenting plan, our attorneys tried to tell us we will renegotiate our document several times over Kelly's childhood years. They said, "Don't worry about school years; you'll cross that bridge when it comes." I think this was generally good advice, for most people anyway. But Mary and I were so oil-and-water back then that it was hard to imagine us agreeing on anything down the road. We needed practical dispute resolution steps that worked. Unfortunately, nothing we wrote ended up working at all for us.

Over the next four years after our initial parenting plan agreement, we had four more legal battles, all primarily due to disputes concerning the visitation schedule that our poorly designed dispute steps failed to help us solve ourselves. We attended a few sessions with professional mediators over that period, but they did nothing for us because the mediators had no authority to make decisions about our problems. It was like going to couples counseling with someone you don't want to be married to—what's the point? We would both dig in our heels and leave the sessions no better off than before.

What Is a Parenting Coordinator?

It was not until when we discovered something called a parenting coordinator that Mary and I finally started working together constructively. It may go by different names in different states, but parenting coordination is essentially a form of binding mediation. The keyword is *binding*. Parent coordination is different from basic mediation in that mediation has no legal authority to impose decisions.

Hopefully, parenting coordination is available in your locality, but if not, you may be able to find someone who does it remotely. It is a voluntary arrangement whereby both parties agree to use a specific mediator as their "parenting coordinator" for a length of time, usually twelve or twenty-four months. At the end of the term, the parties can agree to renew the arrangement or terminate it.

With a parenting coordinator arrangement, you agree to participate in regular mediation sessions, perhaps weekly or monthly, or maybe only "as needed." In these mediation sessions, you and your co-parent hash out your disagreements in a constructive way. The parenting coordinator (I'll call him/her the PC from now on) has the ultimate *legal authority* to settle any disputes, but this is the last thing she wants to do. She aims to help the two of you compromise on your differences. She will intervene with a "must follow" proclamation that has the weight of the law behind it only if there is a situation that endangers the child or if the discussion hits a wall and the two parties are at an impasse over a particular topic, such as where to meet for transitions or how to share holiday time.

For example, if Mary and I were working with a PC during that Christmas vacation argument, we would have skipped all those initial dispute resolution steps and just scheduled an appointment with our PC (or at least written our arguments out in an email if there was no time for a meeting). Our PC would then spend an hour or so trying to bring us to a compromise, and if that didn't happen, she would eventually decide the issue for us. This cuts through all the meaningless steps Mary and I had written in our original parenting plan about contacting a friend or an expert who had no authority to do anything anyway.

When she was not solving disputes for us, our PC spent time hearing our opposing points of view on all sorts of issues and helped us come to practical agreements that just *worked*. For example, when we couldn't agree on where to meet for visit transitions, because I liked to use the Amtrak train and Mary liked to drive, our PC helped us find a creative solution (all meetings to take place at the train station from now on).

Our PC always stressed the value of putting important dates and information in writing so there were no verbal miscommunications. This may sound obvious, but until then, Mary had largely refused to communicate via email with me, so there was always confusion about who, what, where, and when things were supposed to happen. Our PC taught us how to communicate effectively, and she made sure we each did what we said we would do. For example, if Mary needed to "check her calendar and get back to me by Friday" with possible makeup visit dates, then our PC would make sure she followed through on that promise.

In short, our PC was a godsend, in my opinion. But again, signing up for a PC is voluntary, and the legal system cannot force you to use one for more than a few months while you await your trial. If you want one longer-term, then both parties must voluntarily agree to it. This is a shame because it really is a better solution than the legal system, but the law in most states says that you cannot force someone to work outside of the litigation process. You cannot force someone into binding parental coordination if they prefer the traditional legal system. They must volunteer for the PC. They must realize it is a better way forward and then sign on the dotted line to give the PC binding legal authority for a given amount of time.

After four terrible legal battles over four terrible years, Mary finally agreed to use a PC for one year. Our stated goal that year was to rewrite our parenting plan now that Kelly was getting closer to school age. However, we never accomplished that goal, in my opinion, because Mary was not willing to commit to any new parenting plan without the "gun to the head" that a pending trial provided.

After about a year of semi-productive sessions with our PC, Mary was unwilling to renew the arrangement despite making some constructive progress. Even though it was a temporary arrangement, the PC helped us make great leaps in our previously dysfunctional relationship. We are still somewhat dysfunctional, but not nearly as bad as before our year with the PC.

I can't say precisely why Mary refused to renew the PC arrangement. Maybe after a year she just got tired of being told how to do things. Or perhaps she grew sick of our scheduled argument every few weeks. I admit that after a year of sessions, I was growing tired of it too. I realized Mary would probably never sign a rewritten parenting agreement, so frequent meetings started to feel pointless. Still, I wanted to keep the PC arrangement on hand for the next significant dispute that arose. I would have gladly renewed the PC agreement every year going forward if Mary had agreed to keep her on standby.

The result of our year with a PC was that although we are now functioning better than before, we are still far from the relationship you would want to have with your co-parent. We don't follow our old dispute resolution steps anymore because they never worked to begin with. And we don't have a PC anymore because Mary refuses to renew the arrangement.

Unfortunately, now that Kelly is over ten years old, we have settled into a sort of "let's just get through this" existence. It's unfortunate because Kelly is now old enough to realize her parents can't even be in the same room without tension, and there are tools out there like a PC and apps like Our Family Wizard, that can help, but Mary just won't use them anymore.

In contrast, Jess gets along great with Adam's father, Bill. They had one battle in the beginning, and since then, everything has been smooth sailing. They don't follow their old parenting plan much anymore except for the financial terms it laid out. They are one of these co-parents who tossed the agreement aside after a few years and now just do what works for them and their child. They never had to go back to litigation like Mary and I did. They never had a parenting coordinator, nor did they ever exercise formal dispute resolution steps. They just respected each other and made sensible, selfless decisions with Adam's best interest at heart. The idea of paying lawyers to update their out-of-date parenting plan is just silly to them because, well, what's the point? Adam will be eighteen in six short years, and they have been able to solve any dispute that has arisen in the past twelve years just fine.

If you think you can co-exist in harmony with your co-parent like Jess and Bill do, then, by all means, write a generalized parenting plan and don't try to anticipate every conceivable future situation in one document. On the other hand, if you think you are more like Mary and me (oil and water), then you will want to spell out more details in your plan and come up with some dispute steps that solve problems in a timely and efficient manner, unlike our document, which you will read at the end of this chapter.

No matter who you are, the best way to ensure a constructive co-parenting existence that avoids future run-ins with the legal system is to agree to use a binding parenting coordinator. These people are licensed and trained to deal with you fairly and constructively and put your child's needs first. Since that is essentially your end goal, you should have nothing to fear from this arrangement. We strongly recommend everyone write a parenting plan that includes an agreement to use a binding parenting coordinator for at least the first twenty-four months, to be renewed annually after that as needed.

As a side note, if your co-parent simply refuses to sign up for a PC, that doesn't leave you totally on your own. We have already mentioned that anyone going through a baby-out-of-wedlock-situation will need help, especially if they are in a high-conflict situation. Find a good coach, therapist, or other counselor to help you work through the issues you *can* control. It won't be as effective as a PC, but it's better than going it alone. Remember, half the battle is dealing with your *own* emotional responses during this difficult time in your life.

What Is Arbitration?

Arbitration is an alternative dispute resolution path that has gained popularity in recent years as the traditional court system has become totally overloaded with cases in many locations. Like parent coordination, arbitration requires each parent to opt-in to the process. But unlike a PC, arbitration *replaces the entire* litigation process. Basically, arbitration means hiring a private judge to rule on your case in a timely and efficient manner compared to the traditional litigation process.

Jess and I never experienced arbitration firsthand, but it sure does sound preferable to the traditional legal system. Mrs. Big recently achieved the American Academy of Matrimonial Lawyers Family Law Arbitration Certification, which is awarded after rigorous training in the application of arbitration procedures to family law issues. According to her firm's website, the advantages of arbitration include:

- The process provides a convenient and reliable timetable.
- The process is private as compared to the courthouse.
- The parties can choose an arbitrator with knowledge and skills appropriate to the issues in the particular case.
- Arbitrators may craft a decision that is specifically tailored to the case.

Our understanding is that while arbitration used to be reserved for high-income divorce cases, now it is being used for all varieties of family law cases, including baby-out-of-wedlock cases like yours. The price tag for arbitration may look high initially, but it is almost certainly lower than a long, drawn-out traditional battle like the one Mary and I had.

Ask your attorney about the possibility of arbitrating your case as an alternative to the traditional litigation process. Since you were never married, your case should be relatively simple to arbitrate and therefore more affordable than divorce arbitration.

A Sample Consent Order and Parenting Plan

Whether you arbitrate your case or go with traditional litigation, the goal is to develop a parenting plan that works well in real life. When you are writing your parenting plan, you can take two paths based on the type of people you are. You can opt to write something vague and flexible that gives broad guidelines like "We will share all holidays approximately equally," or you can write your agreement in a detailed way, as Mary and I did.

The consent order Mary and I signed is shown below, along with the parenting plan and custody provisions that it refers to. My comments are in italic after some paragraphs that I wished were changed with hindsight. Indeed, much of this document was changed in the four legal battles we had after this first one, in large part because the dispute steps we wrote here were not practical.

Again, I must emphasize the only thing that helped Mary and me through our many problems was our year with a binding parenting coordinator. Please consider adding one to your parenting plan from day one, especially if you anticipate a difficult working relationship with your co-parent.

Also, a reminder about high-conflict situations: while the plan below is detailed, if you are in a high-conflict situation, then the professionals recommend *even more detail* than what you see below. For example, in a high-conflict relationship, you want your document to spell out exactly when and where you pick up and drop off the child each week. High-conflict parents cannot tolerate regular communication the way the rest of us can. If your relationship improves over time, you can always loosen the rules, but you want the detail at first in case you need it. You will want to print and keep a copy of this document with you in your car and your house so you can pull it out quickly if you ever need to show law enforcement or some other authority that you are simply following the agreement.

As usual, we altered or hid some names, dates, and dollar values protect privacy. An actual consent order would show the correct dates and figures in it. The spelling, grammar, and punctuation mistakes you see below are from the original document.

Jim A. Braz, Plaintiff	In the Circuit Court
vs.	For Nameless County, MD
Mary ABC, Defendant	Case No. 1234567

Consent Order

This matter having been scheduled for a two day merits trial on September 16th, 20XY, and the parties with counsel having reached full agreement as to all outstanding issues in the above referenced case, it is this 16th day of September, 20XY, by the Circuit Court for Nameless County,

ORDERED and agreed that the Plaintiff be and hereby is established to be the biological father of the minor child of the parties born Sept X, 20XX; and it is further

ORDERED and agreed that the parties shall share joint legal custody of the minor child, subject to the terms and provisions of the parenting document entitled Custody Provisions, attached hereto and incorporated herein; and it is further

ORDERED and agreed that the Defendant shall have primary physical custody of the minor child, subject to the access rights of Plaintiff as more fully set forth in the parenting document entitled Custody Provisions, attached hereto and incorporated herein; and it is further

ORDERED and agreed that the parties shall share holidays and other vacations and special days as more fully set forth in the parenting document entitled Holidays, attached hereto and incorporated herein; and it is further

ORDERED and agreed that the Plaintiff shall pay child support to Defendant accounting from September 1, 20XY in the amount of X thousand dollars per month and that by agreement of the parties, Plaintiff shall make that payment directly to Defendant. The parties acknowledge that said payment exceeds the extrapolated amount set forth in the Maryland Child Support Guidelines, a copy of which is attached hereto and incorporated herein. Said child support obligation shall continue until the later to occur of the child's 18th birthday or graduation from high school, but in no event shall such payments continue beyond the child's 19th birthday, and it is further

ORDERED and agreed that the Plaintiff shall provide the existing or equivalent health insurance for the minor child, providing that insurance is available through his employer; Plaintiff's obligation for health insurance shall continue until the later to occur of the child's 18th birthday or graduation from high school, but in no event shall such payments continue beyond the child's 19th birthday; and it is further

ORDERED and agreed that the parties shall share the cost of the minor child's uninsured medical expenses and agreed upon extra-curricular activities until such time as the Defendant secures full-time employment, with Plaintiff paying seventy-five percent (75%) and with Defendant paying twenty-five percent (25%) of all such documented expenses; upon the Defendant commencing full-time employment in her selected industry, the parties shall share all uninsured documented medical costs equally; Defendant shall, as a precondition to Plaintiff's contribution to uninsured medical expenses, utilize health insurance plan providers; and it is further

ORDERED and agreed that Defendant hereby waives claim for contribution to averred child support arrearages through September 15th, 20XY and it is further

ORDERED and agreed that Plaintiff shall, by October 1st, 20XY pay to Defendant the sum of Ten Thousand Dollars ($10,000) as and for contribution to Defendant's counsel fees, and upon such payment, Defendant waives all claim to any further contribution to fees incurred through September 15th, 20XY; and it is further

ORDERED and agreed that this matter be and hereby is removed from the trial docket for September 16 and 17, 20XY; and it is further

ORDERED and agreed that Defendant's counter-complaint be and hereby is dismissed, and it is further

ORDERED and agreed that the Plaintiff pay any outstanding costs;

Consented to: (signatures)

Jim A. Braz, Plaintiff   Mrs. P.L. Big, Attorney for Plaintiff

Mary ABC, Defendant   Mr. S.K. Prohn, Attorney for Defendant

John J. Wapner, Judge, Circuit Court for Nameless County, MD

Custody Provisions

The parties agree that they shall have **Joint Legal Custody** of the child and that both are fit and proper persons to share joint legal custody.

1. It is agreed that the parent with whom the child is at any time residing will have day-to-day parental responsibility of the child and each will respect the other's judgment. Each parent recognizes the other has the child's best interests at heart. However, all decisions that have a significant, long term impact on the child (education, health care, etc.) will be made by consensus unless in an emergency situation when the other parent is not able to be reached.

2. Each Parent agrees to utilize constructive problem solving (e.g., negotiation, mediation), as opposed to destructive means (e.g., bad-mouthing, withholding monies/access, etc.).

3. Neither party shall act unilaterally to disturb the child's status quo to implement his/her own decision in any area of the child's health, education, religion, or well being. **Rather, in the event of a disagreement, the following protocol (hereinafter Protocol) will be followed:**

    a. **The issue of disagreement is to be clearly identified by the parties.** *We should have specified "identified in writing via email, so there is a timestamp of the beginning of the dispute."*

    b. **The parties shall use good faith and reasonable efforts to persuade each other** of the correctness of their respective positions. *We should have spec-*

ified a timeline, such as "within one week of initiating the dispute in writing via step (a) or sooner if the situation requires a faster resolution."

c. If a disagreement persists, the **parties shall identify an expert** in the field of disagreement to assist them in resolving their differences (i.e. a pediatrician for health care, a guidance counselor for education, etc.) *We should have specified what happens once we identify that person or else folded this step into another step.*

d. If a disagreement still persists, the parties shall in good faith **consult an individual known to both of them** within whom trust is reposed, and said individual shall act as a mediator in attempting to assist the parties in resolving their disputes. *We should have dropped this all together. We used a mutual friend once (actually, it was one of Mary's friends, as we didn't have any genuinely mutual friends). She hated being forced to take sides and, therefore, didn't help much. This step doesn't work well in real life.*

e. If a disagreement persists further, the parties shall **employ the services of a professional mediator** of their choosing or failing that, chosen by their counsel. The cost of mediation shall be divided equally between the parties. The mediator shall be permitted to testify only as to the good faith efforts of each party in attempting to resolve the dispute. All other confidences surrounding mediation shall remain in force and effect. *This is okay, better than nothing, but falls short of what you will need because mediators are not timely and they do not have binding authority. As we emphasized previously,* *only a binding parenting coordinator can step in quickly and solve a dispute in real-time for you. When Mary and I tried to use this step in real life, we first argued over the choice of mediator and then the date of mediation. In the end, we disregarded the mediator's recommendation, entrenching ourselves firmly in our respective corners.*

f. **Finally, if an agreement still cannot be had, and all the above steps have been completed in good faith, Ms. Mary may have the final say in all disputes except for those concerning the following subjects**: *If you have joint legal custody, you should not want to give up final say in all disputes because every argument will end in "Well, I have the final say, so there's nothing more to talk about." If someone must have the final say, make it a parenting coordinator.*

    i. Any decision concerning any aspect of the access schedule (including transportation, holidays and vacations, locations of visits, duration of visits, or any other term pertaining to conditions of access). *Obviously, I wasn't giving Mary the final say on these issues.*

    ii. Any decision that would commit Mr. Braz to expenses beyond those set forth in the Consent Order incorporating this document, or any expense set forth in this document. *Also important for obvious reasons.*

    iii. Any major medical decision concerning the child's long term well-being.

iv. Mother shall have the final say regarding all education decisions except that she may not enroll the child in a religious school without the Father's consent. *I should have worried more about homeschooling than religious schooling.*

g. In the event of a disagreement between the parties as to any issue set forth above in paragraphs numbered (f) (1-4), the dispute resolution Protocol steps "a" through "e" will be followed.

4. **Both parents will act with the intention of creating peace and harmony for each other and the child by recognizing and respecting the following:**

a. Neither parent will criticize or demean the other or the other's family either in or out of the child's presence. *If this isn't obvious, it should be. Your child does not want to hear you bad-mouth their other parent, period.*

b. Both parents agree to go directly to the other parent for information and to refrain from putting the child, the child's relatives, or any other individual in the middle of parental communication, including electronic communication such as email. *This is important; don't put anyone in the middle of communication with your co-parent, especially not your child.*

c. Neither parent shall do anything which may estrange the child from the other parent or hamper the natural and continuing relationship between the child and the other parent. The use of the term "Mom" and "Dad" are only to be used with the child's natural parents. *This last sentence goes without saying, I think, but Mary wanted it.*

d. Each will respect time schedules and be prompt. When this is not possible, notice shall be given as soon as possible to alert the other as to lateness and the reason. *This issue has caused Mary and me countless arguments since I'm always early and she is usually late. It's a nice paragraph, but I can't say it did much to make Mary more punctual. Some people just don't respect time, and others do. There is not much you can do about punctuality except to arrange that the parent getting the child always "picks up," ideally from a third party like the daycare center. Mary is rarely late when she receives Kelly but almost never on time when she is dropping her off to me.*

e. Each parent shall notify the other immediately upon making, scheduling, or receiving any medical, mental health, or dental appointment for the child and shall further provide the other parent with full information about the time, date, name, and address of the provider with whom the appointment is scheduled. *This has proved to be important over the years; make sure to include this.*

f. Each parent will notify the other immediately as to any medical emergency concerning the child that arises while under their supervision. *Obvious but important.*

g. Both parties shall be listed on all school and medical forms as parents. Neither party shall move the child from her school (either permanently or temporarily) without the full knowledge and consent of the other. *Important, but in practice, when my daughter misses school, I usually hear about it after the fact, which is better than not hearing about it at all. Also important to emphasize that the choice of which school to attend is a major decision that should be made by consensus for parents with joint legal custody.*

h. Both parents shall be entitled to attend all school, church, medical, or extracurricular activities, events, and appointments in which either child participates or of which the child is subject. Each parent shall make copies for and promptly provide to the other every notice, report card, progress report, calendar of events/activities, school calendar, or other information provided to him/her by the school. *Also important, so definitely include this.*

i. Each parent will be responsible and prompt with any payments, information, and materials due to the other parent. *Definition of prompt?*

j. The parties agree that the child's religion shall be "XYZ"; and that each will respect the child's religion and practices; however, neither party is required to ensure that the child attends weekly church services or religious classes during their time with the child. *Religion might or might not be important to you, but you typically cannot force anyone to attend religious services during their time with the child.*

k. Each parent shall have sole decision-making rights concerning their choice of childcare/nanny/babysitter if needed while the child is in their physical custody, subject to the Right of First Refusal clause set forth below. *The confusing right of first refusal clause below was included because Mary was concerned I would leave Kelly with a nanny, grandparents, or babysitter during my visitation time. After a lot of back and forth, we adopted the following language.*

l. "Right of First Refusal" clause: During either party's access with the child, in the event that the custodial parent is unable to personally care for the child for a period of more than eight (8) hours, the non-custodial parent shall have the right of first refusal and shall be entitled to care for the child in the other parent's absence, above all third party caregivers until the child reaches age twenty-four (24) months. Once the child reaches twenty-four (24) months of age, both parties' parents may care for the child overnight in the party's stead on three occasions during each calendar year. The parties agree in the year 20XX+4 to discuss the expansion of the child's stays with the paternal grandparents, using the dispute resolution protocol. It is the parties' intention to foster a close relationship between the minor child and both sets of grandparents. *This long, confusing paragraph tried to balance Mary's concerns about me leaving Kelly with someone in my place with my concerns about letting my parents use some of my alone time with Kelly. As it turned out, neither of our concerns ended up mattering. My advice looking back is to keep it simple and just allow each parent to do what they want with their visitation time. Remember, if you are always giving your visitation time to a third-party caretaker, it may not help your cause if you have to return to the courts in the future.*

m. The child's belongings and clothing shall at all times be made available to the child, regardless of the parent in whose home they are spending time. All clothing and toys, books, sporting equipment, or other belongings that are sent with the child to the home of the one parent shall be returned with the child to the home of the other parent. *Hopefully, neither you nor your co-parent would try to monopolize your child's toys. I don't think this paragraph is necessary for a legal document, but it doesn't hurt either.*

n. Each parent shall, during his/her time with the child, afford the other at least once daily telephone contact with the child. Messages from the other parent, and from the child, shall be conveyed and returned promptly. The child herself may call the other parent upon request and when old enough to do so. *I didn't realize it at the time, but a daily phone call is especially important when you are the visiting parent. The calls should be brief (fifteen minutes max), initiated by the parent caring for the child, and part of the daily routine. Video calls are especially helpful for young children.*

o. Each party shall afford the other 90 days written notice via email of any intended change of address more than 25 miles from any major Amtrak station, including or between Union Station in Washington, D.C. and Penn Station in New York City, NY. *This was probably unnecessary because each state has rules on notifying the other parent about changes of address. Still, it was good for us to put something in writing to ensure we both understood notifications were required. We will discuss relocating more in the last chapter.*

5. Access Schedule

The Father shall have the child with him according to the terms set forth herein below: *This is the extremely long, four-step, twelve-month phase-in described previously. This is not typical! Your phase-in should be much shorter if you have one at all.*

a. **Phase 1** — September 15, 20XY until December 17, 20XY (age 12-15 months)

   i. Any number of hours (but not overnight) on any Saturday or Sunday in his parent's home town in Pennsylvania (with at least 7 days notice via email).

   ii. Upon at least seven days' notice via email from Mother, Father shall spend at least 5 hours in MD on any weekend that Mother does not wish to travel to Pennsylvania (where Father's parents reside) during this phase, provided at least two of every four weekends include visits in Pennsylvania.

   iii. Restrictions apply: Mother may do all the long-distance driving if she wishes; Father may drive the child in his Pennsylvania home town only; Father must be present for all hours with the child; During this phase, he shall have no special holiday access with the child.

b. **Phase 2** — December 18th, 20XY until June 10, 20XZ (age 15 -21 months)

   i. Father shall have at least 24-hour visits in Father's home town from Noon Saturday until Noon Sunday every other weekend beginning Saturday, December 18th, 20XY.

   ii. Mother may at her sole election attend the first overnight in Father's home if she chooses. *Mary chose not to attend.*

   iii. Increase the hours every other weekend in Father's home town at Mother's discretion; however, 46-hour visits shall begin on June 10th, 20XZ.

   iv. Father may spend at least one additional 5-hour visit with the child in MD per calendar month at his option, on a date mutually agreed and with at least 7 days notice in advance via email.

v. Restrictions apply: Mother may do all the long-distance driving if she wishes; Father may drive the child in his home town in PA only; Father must be present for all hours with the child, Holiday Schedule set forth hereinbelow shall pertain, but the duration of any holiday access shall be limited by the greatest number of consecutive hours reached so far.

c. **Phase 3** — June 10th, 20XZ until September 13th, 20XZ (age 21-24 months)

i. At least 46-hour visits from 7 pm Friday until 5 pm Sunday every other weekend in either Father's parents' home town in PA or his parents' vacation home in Nameless Beach Town, New Jersey.

ii. Father may spend at least one other 5-hour visit in MD per calendar month at his option, on a date mutually agreed and with at least 7 days notice in advance via email.

iii. Mother shares in all the long-distance traveling burden equally unless otherwise agreed on, up to a limit of the distance between Washington, DC to Nameless Beach Town, NJ.

iv. Regular holiday schedule begins without restriction or limitation.

v. Restrictions apply: Father shall be present for all hours with the child; Father shall conduct all visits in his parent's home town in PA or Nameless Beach Town, NJ only.

d. **Phase 4 — Permanent Schedule** — Sept 13th, 20XZ (age 24 months)

   i. Identical to Phase 3 above except the geographic restrictions are lifted and Mother shares all the long-distance traveling burden equally unless otherwise agreed upon, up to a limit of the distance from Washington, DC to New York, NY. Any distance beyond that is the responsibility of the party wishing to travel further away during their time with the child. At such time as the Father begins visits with the minor child at his residence, he shall assure that there no safety covenants in force and effect, prohibiting children from residing in his building. *The provisions about sharing the travel burden "equally" were very important to us, and I suggest everyone includes it in their plan. Additionally, one of the issues addressed in one of our follow-up legal battles was that Mary would not allow my parents to participate in transitions (i.e., she wouldn't drop off Kelly with her grandparents). We recommend you include language on exactly who is allowed to pick up and drop off the child, including grandparents, nannies, etc.*

   ii. No restrictions as set forth hereinabove shall apply.

6. Holidays

    a.   The Parties shall alternate the following holidays: New Year's Day; Martin Luther King Day; Presidents' Day; Memorial Day, July 4th (noon on July 4th until noon on July 5th); and Labor Day. *One-day holidays are useless, especially when you have a long distance to travel. We should have designated "Monday holidays" like MLK to include the adjacent weekends and single days like July 4th to be at least forty-eight hours long.*

    b.   The Parties agree that the Father shall have the child on Martin Luther King Day, Memorial Day, and Labor Day in all even-numbered years and shall have New Year's Day, Presidents' Day, and July 4th in all odd-numbered years.

    c.   Conversely, Mother shall have the child on Martin Luther King Day, Memorial Day, and Labor day in all odd-numbered years and shall have New Year's Day, Presidents' Day, and July 4th in all even-numbered years.

We were trying to spread the holidays evenly across the year, but it made life very difficult because my alternating weekends sometimes fell adjacent to my holiday and sometimes adjacent to her holiday. We often had to reschedule a regular weekend visit to make it work, and each of those discussions led to other arguments about when the rescheduled weekend would take place. Everything would have been much easier and worked out evenly in the long term if we just wrote that any of those holidays that fell adjacent to my regular weekend were automatically added to my regular weekend schedule, creating occasional long weekends a few times a year. Holidays that landed adjacent to Mary's weekends would stay with her. While there would be some stretches of months that one parent or the other got more holidays, it would balance out over the long term. If we had done it that way, we would have avoided dozens of arguments about how to move the calendar around to accommodate holidays. The less you need to discuss modifying the schedule going forward, the better. You can do it this way while still making special rules for the most significant holidays like Christmas, Thanksgiving, and spring break.

d. Except as set forth to the contrary or otherwise agreed to by the parties, the holidays identified hereinabove shall occur from 6 pm the day before the holiday until 6 pm the day of the holiday. If the party is scheduled for a Friday or Monday holiday occurring contiguously to that party's standard alternating weekend with the child, the weekend shall be extended to occur without interruption through the holiday, including Christmas and the spring / Easter break described below. *Twenty-four-hour holidays are no good. We should have made sure long weekends stayed that way.*

e. Thanksgiving shall consist of two blocks of time to be alternated between the parties from year to year. Block A shall commence at 5 pm on the Wednesday before Thanksgiving and continue until 5 pm on Friday; Block B shall commence at 5 pm on Friday and continue until Sunday evening at 5 pm. Father shall have Block A in all even-numbered years and Block B in all odd-numbered years; conversely, Mother shall have Block A in all odd-numbered years and Block B in all even-numbered years. *Splitting Thanksgiving into two blocks worked okay for us. However, remember when one parent has physical custody and the other visits a few days a month, you really only need to spell out the visiting parent's holiday rights. It would have been simpler just to say, "Father gets Thanksgiving from 5:00 p.m. Wednesday night to 5:00 p.m. Friday night in all even-numbered years." That framework would have probably been cleaner for all the holidays since there is no need to spell out both schedules if you think about it.*

f. Christmas shall consist of two blocks of time, to be alternated between the parties from year to year. Block A shall commence at noon on December 24th and continue until noon on Christmas Day; Block B shall commence at noon on Christmas Day and continue to noon on December 26th. Father shall have Block B in all even-numbered years and Block A in all odd-numbered years; conversely, Mother shall have Block B in all odd-numbered years and Block A in all even-numbered years. The parties shall extend the Father's Christmas access period commencing in 20XX+4 and shall utilize the dispute resolution protocol for doing so in the event they are unable to agree. *Again, there are better ways to write this. And again, one-day holidays are useless. Christmas is hard because everyone wants to wake up with the child on Christmas morning. We tried to slice Christmas day in half, and it ruined it each year because we had to be on the road by 10:00 am to get to the other parent. With hindsight, I would have preferred to alternate a forty-eight-hour Christmas block each year instead. We eventually expanded my Christmas holiday with our parenting coordinator. Now, we split Kelly's school winter break evenly down the middle each year and alternate the good half (the one with Christmas).*

g. Spring / Easter Break: The parties agree that every year the child will be with Mother on Easter Sunday beginning on Saturday at noon prior to Easter Sunday to attend church service. The parties further agree that every year Father shall have the child during the Good Friday holiday from 10 am Friday until noon Saturday. The parties shall extend Father's Spring / Easter break commencing in 20XY+4, and shall utilize the dispute resolution protocol for doing so in the event they are unable to agree. *Once school started, and with our parenting coordinator's help, we began to split the spring break week in half. Kelly always comes with me for the first half and with Mary for the second half, including Easter Sunday. Again, the short, twenty-six-hour Good Friday holiday as it is written here is not very useful. Better to split the entire spring break week from year one, even if the child will not be in school for a number of years.*

h. Mother's Day, Father's Day, Birthdays: The parties agree that the child shall always be with the

Mother on Mother's Day and with the Father on Father's Day for at least 8 hours. The parties agree that on the child's birthdays, the regular schedule shall be followed but that the other parent may participate for up to three hours on the child's birthday, or during any birthday celebrations/parties which include the child's peers as guests. *This paragraph might have worked fine if we lived nearby each other, but we didn't. I would prefer to celebrate Father's Day on another day if it didn't fall on my regular weekend. However, Mary felt strongly about Mother's Day, so we included this provision, and now we usually have to move around one or two weekends to accommodate it. Remember, every time you have to alter the regular weekend schedule, it is a potential argument about when to move it. The birthday party provision was never really used; in reality, Kelly has had two parties most years, one with Mom and one with me. Perhaps it would make better sense as it was written if we lived nearby each other and maintained an overlapping circle of friends, but we don't.*

All holidays and special days described here shall supercede the regular access schedule, with no compensation or adjustment to the regular schedule. *This is important to spell out to make sure everyone understands. If your holiday falls on my regularly scheduled weekend, then, I lose my time without makeup. We should have included some language about makeups due to illness, bad weather, or whatever other reasons, but I suppose we just figured we would use the dispute resolution steps.*

7. Summer Vacation

a. The Parties agree on the following summer vacation schedule to afford the father time with the child that is uninterrupted by time with the mother. *This makes sense to me, but Mary later expressed that she wanted the right to choose summer vacation time with Kelly that was uninterrupted by visits with me. I still don't understand that thinking since her sole physical custody affords her twenty-four out of every twenty-eight nights in a typical month with Kelly, or approximately 85% of the time.*

b. 20XZ (Age 20 months, during phase 3 of the access phase-in) — a total of 7 days, to be exercised in blocks resulting in no more than three consecutive overnights, which blocks shall not interfere with Mother's regularly scheduled weekends with the child. Each block shall be exercised in July or August.

c. 20XA (Age 32 months) — a total of 10 days, to be exercised in blocks resulting in no more than four consecutive overnights, which blocks shall not interfere with Mother's regularly scheduled weekends with the child.

d. 20XB (Age 44 months) — a total of 14 days, consisting of blocks resulting in no more than 7 consecutive nights, which block shall not interfere with Mother's regularly scheduled weekends with the child. No block shall occur during the month of July without the Mother's consent. *Mary wanted to travel for a long period each summer with Kelly, but she must have forgotten I'd still have my regular weekends in July unless I agreed to move them.*

e. 20XC (Age 56 months) and beyond — the parties shall expand Father's vacation days for 20XC and beyond; they shall attempt agreement using the same dispute resolution protocol as set forth herein. *The expansion of summer vacation time never happened. Despite several follow-up lawsuits and many mediation sessions, Mary has rarely granted me more than fourteen vacation days in the summer. This is curious because many would argue the visiting parent should have the majority of the summer because they get so little during the school year, but Mary never saw it this way, and it is one battle I have just stopped fighting due to fatigue.*

f. Father shall notify Mother by April 1st of each year in writing via email as to his selected summer access dates. Selection shall override all plans, camps, and other access of the Mother (except for the Mother's regularly scheduled weekends and holiday rights described in the Holiday Schedule for Memorial Day, July 4th, and Labor Day which are dictated by the holiday schedule) provided notice is afforded in accordance with the terms set forth herein. Father's failure of timely notice to Mother shall not abrogate his right to summer access, but shall subordinate such access periods to the Mother's summer vacation, schedule of camps and activities for the child.

So, the father picks his vacation days by April 1st each year—pretty simple, right? Wrong. Each of the first four years after this agreement was signed, I submitted my chosen days by April 1st to Mary, and each year she refused to accept them, stating one disagreement or another. Some years she didn't like that I had single vacation days spread over the summer adjacent to my regular weekends. Other years, she didn't like that I had too many consecutive days in a row, despite the language addressing that above. Every year she claimed she had some say in the days I chose because there were things she wanted to do with Kelly in the summer too, the big one being a six-week trip to the West Coast each summer.

Summer vacation disputes were at the heart of our four follow-up legal confrontations, including two binding mediation arrangements. Vacation scheduling shouldn't be so difficult, but it has been a massive heartache for me year after year. Mary and I even argued in future litigation about the definition of the words "summer" and "day," so it is wise to include as much detail as you can here. I recommend you make sure you have a date in the spring when the summer schedule needs to be finalized and ensure you have a mechanism in place, preferably a parenting coordinator, to help you solve summer vacation disputes. Mary would say it is best to give both parties some say in choosing the days; perhaps you alternate first choices each summer or in some other equitable rotation.

7 | Financial and Child Support Questions

When confronted with an unexpected pregnancy, it is natural to be concerned about how much the child will cost. First, remember what my cousin said to me a long time ago: "Don't worry so much. All they really need is love." Your newborn will come into the world knowing nothing of brand-name baby clothes, expensive luxury gear, or extravagant vacations. All they really need is love, food, and a safe place to sleep, so try not to panic too much about money.

Sure, diapers add up, but you won't need to rent a larger apartment or buy a bigger car anytime soon. Babies themselves are basically low cost, and child support should be manageable. However, it's the attorney's fees that can get you in trouble. Try to look on the bright side; if you were getting divorced, it would be much more expensive. You would be splitting your assets down the middle and possibly paying alimony in addition to child support.

Alimony is a payment made from one spouse to another after a divorce for a limited number of years to help equalize the standard of living for each party after the divorce. For this book, we will assume you were not married to your co-parent, and therefore there is no alimony involved. For baby-out-of-wedlock situations like yours, you only have to think about child support and attorney's fees, and we will look at both of them in this chapter.

Child Support Calculations

When I first met Mrs. Big, one of my first questions was to ask how much child support I would owe Mary. I told her a few details about my income, which was a lot more than Mary was making as an executive assistant before quitting her job. I guessed at the time I would be paying her $1,000–$2,000 a month in child support. I remember being very confused in that meeting when Mrs. Big told me I would probably owe significantly more than that.

You might be asking, like I was, "Surely babies don't cost two thousand dollars a month?" True. But the calculation is not based on what they cost. Child support calculations are primarily based on one parent's income relative to the other parent's income. Let us say that again, so it sinks in: what counts the most is your income, not the child's expenses.

Before we go further, we must explain that every state has a different formula for child support calculation. Some states are "generous" to the parent with physical custody, and some are not. And some, like Maryland, change their laws from time to time. In the first few years of Kelly's life, the Maryland state legislature changed their support calculations such that they went from being one of the stingiest states in the country to one of the most generous. Lucky timing for Mary; she got the amount revised higher soon after the laws changed.

Although the support calculations are mostly based on income, your expenses do factor in to some degree. You will likely have to describe (and prove with documents) your recent expenses, as well as your income. In Maryland and Pennsylvania, for example, Jess and I each had to fill out a lengthy expense sheet that showed what our typical bills were, such as rent, utilities, car payment, credit cards, etc.

I did not understand why I had to show the court my expenses if all they cared about was my income. The answer was that they wanted to make sure I didn't have any special needs. For example, perhaps I was paying child support to another woman, or maybe I cared for my elderly mother. Pricey daycare or a nanny could move the calculation a lot, probably. Certainly, they would want to know if our child had an expensive medical condition.

Anyway, you will probably have to disclose your income and your expenses over the past several years. The way it works is the judge/attorneys input the numbers into the state's software program. The program compares income and expenses between the two parties and spits out an amount that (typically) the visiting parent pays to the parent with physical custody each month. If you have 50/50 joint physical custody, then all the system is comparing is relative wealth, because the expense of caring for the child is split evenly. All the attorneys have access to this financial software in advance, so one thing you are paying them for is to calculate this child support number using their software.

If there is a single website that gives child support calculations for every state in the union, we cannot find it. The online calculators we have seen are usually inaccurate. I recently tried plugging my numbers into one of these websites, and it gave me a completely incorrect result. My guess is some states make the information easy to find, and others just don't. There is probably no single source of reliable information for every state in the country.

My situation was relatively simple at the time of our custody battle. I had an income. Mary had none, and no one, including our child, had any extraordinary expenses like a medical condition or even a nanny. After a lot of trial and error with my lawyer, I pieced together a rule of thumb that told me my *monthly* child support payment in Maryland would be approximately 1% of my *annual* pre-tax income. Annualized, you could say I paid about 12% of my pre-tax income in child support as the visiting parent. The amount would have been less if I had joint physical custody because then I would have been shouldering more of Kelly's expenses.

So, for example, if I made about $100,000 a year before taxes and Mary earned zero, then I would owe her about $1,000 a month ($12,000 a year) in child support. If I made $200,000 a year, I would owe her about $2,000 a month ($24,000 a year) in support. Importantly, child support income is tax-free to the parent receiving it, but not tax deductible for the parent paying it. Since I was in a high-income tax bracket in a high tax location (Manhattan), I was paying out over 20% of my annual take-home pay (after-tax pay) in child support.

By contrast, Jessica was working when she and Bill had their child support numbers calculated by their attorneys. The difference with them is they were in Pennsylvania rather than Maryland, and they were both working, so the formula was slightly different than if one parent had zero income. We don't know the exact numbers, but Jess believes both her and Bill were making about $50,000 annually at the time. Importantly, Jess had her son in daycare so she could work, and therefore Bill had to contribute a significant amount to that expense, which pushed up his total number owed to her. When it was all factored in, Bill ended up owing about $1,275 a month ($15,300 a year), which worked out to about 30% of his annual pre-tax income if it is true he was making about $50,000 at the time.

If you want another complication to consider, let me tell you that at one point, Mary was planning to move out of Maryland. I asked Mrs. Big what would happen to my child support calculation if Mary moved out of state. I was told no matter where she went, the new controlling jurisdiction would be New York State because I was staying put there.

So I talked to some family law attorneys in New York, and they told me New York had a cap on child support of $5,000 a month, no matter how much money you made. Maryland had no such cap. However, while Maryland law said child support was to be paid until age eighteen, in New York it was paid until age twenty-one. Since she never moved, none of this mattered in the end for me, but we want to make sure you understand whether your state has a cap on payments and at what age the payments end.

We don't have any experience with 50/50 physical custody, but we're sure that arrangement would lessen the payment further from the higher-income spouse to the lower-income spouse. Obviously, if your child lives with you half the time, you have about half the expenses to shoulder, so there would be less reason to pay the lower-income parent as much.

Which begs the question I asked Mrs. Big on day one: "Surely babies don't cost two thousand dollars a month?" True, they don't. And your child's expenses might be fully covered without you paying the custodial parent anything at all. But it's not about just expenses. The fact is that in most states, the law is designed to *partially equalize* the living standards of both parents. The keyword is partially—not fully—equalize.

Whereas alimony is meant to *nearly equalize* living standards after a divorce, child support payments from the higher-income to the lower-income parent are intended to balance it only *partially*. Child support aims to make sure the child doesn't live in a slum with one parent on the weekdays and in a mansion with the other parent on the weekends. It could also be the other way around. Suppose the parent with physical custody is a celebrity making $100 million a year, and the visiting parent is a regular Joe. In that case, you can imagine the visiting parent might be the one getting paid child support.

It's enough to make your head spin, and it is all very confusing. The bottom line is you will need your attorney to plug the income and expense numbers into your state's calculator and see what it says. In our experience, an estimate would be that the visiting parent pays something like 10–30% of their annual pre-tax income to the custodial parent. However, there are lots of moving parts, so don't make any assumptions without talking to your attorney.

More about Child Support Calculations

The discussion above assumes you have perfect information on the inputs to the calculations. That is, you know exactly what your income and your co-parent's income is. But for many of us, income can vary widely for both legitimate and illegitimate reasons. For example, if you work in sales and get paid on commission, you might have good years or bad years. I worked on Wall Street, and most of my income came in an annual bonus lump sum that varied widely from year to year. These would be legitimate reasons your income varies.

If you are a waiter or bartender, you probably earn a large percent of your income in cash tips that are likely underreported on your tax returns and pay stubs. If you own your own small business, you may be incentivized to "cook the books" to make it looks less profitable for income tax and child support calculations. These would be illegitimate reasons your income varies from year to year.

To get to the truth, you will be asked to show several years of income and expense history so the court can determine an average level of income. If they looked at only one calendar year, some people might try to play games by diverting some of their income into the last year or next year's pay period. Expect to be asked for at least three years' worth of tax returns, pay stubs, credit cards, bank statements, investment accounts, and your business financial records; it's all fair game.

Even gifts or inheritance from your wealthy uncle can count as income. If the opposing attorney is any good, they will leave no stone unturned to ensure you are not hiding anything. I remember being asked for my mortgage application documents because when you apply for credit, you are not likely to make yourself look poorer than you really are.

Be truthful from day one about your income and expenses because you are not likely to get away with anything. If you are caught trying to hide something, you can be sure the judge will hold it against you in a trial.

You may be thinking it is not fair to calculate child support payments once and have them fixed at that level for the next eighteen years since your income may legitimately change over the years. You are correct. Child support payments can be changed over time as circumstances change. We will come back to this topic later in this chapter.

In many cases, the parties are wise enough to compromise on legal custody, visitation rights, and a parenting plan, but they get stuck on the child support number. Your attorney might say you should get X while the other attorney thinks your co-parent should only pay Y. If you cannot compromise on the number, then sometimes the parties will go to trial, asking the judge just to settle this one last remaining item.

While not preferable to a full settlement, this kind of partial settlement is better than nothing because at least you get a customized parenting plan rather than the judge's "off the shelf" plan. The money issue will be settled easily enough by the judge. Just remember, you may be haggling over a few hundred dollars a month, which equals only a few thousand dollars a year. Is that worth the tens of thousands in legal bills you may pay in preparing for a trial? Is it worth the stress of a trial? Do yourself a favor and just compromise down the middle on the child support number if it means avoiding a trial.

One last comment about child support payments. People who pay them almost always feel they are too high, and people who receive them almost always feel they are too low. Like any good negotiation, this mutual unhappiness means it is a fair outcome. When I told my colleagues in Manhattan how much child support I was paying, I got the same reaction time and time again. At first, they were surprised at how high the number was, but on further reflection, they all said it was a lot less than their wives spent each month on the family credit card! That is probably a sexist comment, but I still find it useful when discussing child support with visiting fathers like me.

Medical Expenses and Extracurricular Activities

Generally, if you are not married or domestic partners, your health insurance will cover your child and yourself but not your co-parent. When Kelly was born, Mary's insurance covered Mary's hospital bills, and my insurance covered Kelly's. We used my insurance for Kelly because it was a better plan, and it was provided by my employer with little extra cost to add my daughter. You'll want to sort out the health insurance issues with your co-parent before the birth, and you will want to notify your insurance company within a day or two of your child's birth to make sure everything is adequately covered. Just give the insurance company a call, and they will walk you through the steps.

If you looked closely at my consent order and parenting agreement in the last chapter, you would have noticed the paragraph that addressed uninsured medical expenses and extracurricular activities:

> **"ORDERED and agreed** that the parties shall share the cost of the minor child's uninsured medical expenses and agreed upon extra-curricular activities until such time as the Defendant secures full-time employment, with Plaintiff paying seventy-five percent (75%) and with Defendant paying twenty-five percent (25%) of all such documented expenses; upon the Defendant commencing full-time employment in her selected industry, the parties shall share all uninsured documented medical costs equally; Defendant shall, as a precondition to Plaintiff's contribution to uninsured medical expenses, utilize health insurance plan providers; and it is further…"

This is a reasonably self-explanatory but essential paragraph in any parenting plan. Every child will have occasional uninsured medical expenses even if they are just doctor co-pays. Unfortunately, your child may have much bigger uninsured medical bills for one reason or another. Any decent lawyer or judge who reviews your agreement will want to make sure this possibility is addressed. The exact split, in my case 75/25, can be negotiated like everything else, but generally, it should fall somewhat in line with your relative incomes. Mary probably could have gotten more than 75% from me and certainly more than the 50% she agreed to once she found employment, but I have never held her to that 50/50 split even after she found full-time employment.

Extracurricular activities are lumped in here, but Mary gives me an easy time with these in practice. She signs Kelly up for all sorts of activities like tennis and piano lessons and never asks me to contribute to them. I suppose the keyword in our language is "agreed-upon" extracurricular activities. Mary doesn't want to haggle with me over it any more than I do, so she usually just pays these relatively minor bills out of my regular support payments.

Jessica's agreement with Bill has a useful minimum clause that exempts all small uninsured or extracurricular bills from reimbursement. For them, any single expense under fifty dollars is exempt from reimbursement because it's just not worth the discussion. You want to save your energy for conversations that matter with your co-parent, and asking for a portion of a doctor's co-pay tends to just feel like nickel-and-dime stuff to everyone involved. We recommend you include something similar in your agreement.

You will also notice a paragraph in the consent order that addresses health insurance. Again, the lawyers and judges will want any agreement to spell out who is paying for health insurance. If the other parent chooses to use doctors outside the child's health insurance network, your agreement should state they alone are responsible for the resulting bills.

Private School and College Savings

You might be wondering why my parenting plan did not mention private school or saving for college. You are welcome to address both in your plan, but consider the following discussion before you do. For me, it was negotiated that Mary would have the final say in all educational decisions with the exception that she could not make a decision that compelled me to pay extra out of pocket, so there was not much left to say about the possibility of a private K–12 school.

In other words, if Mary wanted to send Kelly to the most expensive private school in Washington, DC, it would be on her dime unless I agreed to contribute. This language seemed like a fair trade-off to me. Of course, if I wanted to push for a more expensive school, there would be nothing stopping me from contributing extra to help persuade Mary to do so, but neither of us could force the other to spend more than was laid out in the agreement.

As for college, in most states that we know of, there is not a requirement for either parent to contribute to a college savings plan. We suppose you could include it as part of your negotiations. Perhaps you could agree to receive less in child support with the condition that the other parent pays into a college savings trust fund each month. We don't recommend this for a few reasons.

First, if you are saving for college or private K–12 schooling, you will want to use a taxed advantage plan called a 529 education savings plan. These plans name a *beneficiary*, who is the child headed to school, but the *owner* of the account is the adult who sets it up. The *owner* has ultimate legal authority over the money; they can give it to another child or withdrawal it prematurely and spend it at the casino if they want to pay the early withdrawal penalty.

Therefore, even if there is a 529 plan with your child named as the beneficiary, the money is never really safe in there if you are not the owner of the account. To make sure it goes only to your child, you must be the owner of the 529 plan or else you would need to put the money in some sort of irrevocable trust, but then it doesn't have the 529 tax advantages. Perhaps you could find a lawyer to help you achieve both goals, but now you're paying another lawyer.

And second, your child may never end up going to college or private school for one reason or another, and then who gets the money that was diverted from your child support payment for years?

Here is a better solution. Keep college savings out of the parenting plan. Open your own 529 plan with you as the owner and your child as the beneficiary. Encourage your co-parent to do the same. Each of you contributes what you can to the respective accounts. Have a discussion about how your child will pay for school if there is not enough money in the 529 plans. This way, if your child doesn't end up ever going to college, then you can give your account to another child or use it for something else—after all, it's your money. If your co-parent doesn't save anything for the child's college, well, shame on them, but most state laws say they are not required to contribute anything.

The *last thing* you want to do is agree to receive a lesser support payment in exchange for your co-parent funding a 529 plan. In this case, your co-parent can run off with the money at the last moment, or your child may never go to college, and then you will be kicking yourself with almost no recourse except another hard-to-win, expensive legal battle.

Payment Mechanisms and Enforcement

If you are purposely withholding payments to get your way in some other dispute, maybe because your visitation time is not being honored, the court will come down hard on you for not doing your part. Two wrongs don't make a right. Mrs. Big always drilled it into my head that no matter how frustrated I was by Mary's lack of compliance with our parenting plan, I should never withhold payment of child support. She wanted to make sure her client would be squeaky clean if we ever ended up in front of a judge.

Once a child support amount is determined, there is no escaping it. If you are late, the overdue amounts will accrue. We are aware of three child support payment mechanisms, and they all result in strict enforcement.

The two most common payment mechanisms are as follows. Either you pay the support directly to your co-parent with a check or electronic transfer of your choosing, or you pay a state collection agency, and they, in turn, transfer the money to the receiving parent. Mary and I use the first method, and there is nothing wrong with it as long as the person paying is punctual with their payments. But if you have the choice and your state offers the service, we recommend signing up for the second method.

In some states, there is no choice in the matter. The state collection agency is the only method some courts will allow. Jess and Bill use the state-run system in Pennsylvania, and we have seen firsthand how well it works. There is a simple website that keeps a running tally of all Bill's payments. Years ago, the court ruled that Bill owed some back payments. Rather than make him pay it all in a lump sum, they spread out the arrears by tacking on a small additional amount to each monthly support number. There is no need for Jess to haggle with Bill over his payments. Everyone can see a clear payment history on the Pennsylvania state website, and we know that eventually, the whole number, including arrears, will be paid off because the state system will never let him get away with missing one dime.

The do-it-yourself method is not as good because, although you can pull up your bank statements in a trial to prove what money was paid or not paid, who wants to get in a dispute about that? Over eighteen years, it's easy to lose track of payments, especially if the payor starts falling behind by more than a month. The state-run system will seamlessly track everything, and that makes enforcement seamless too.

When Jess and I first started dating, she struggled financially because Bill was frequently late paying his support. Some months he was so late it amounted to not paying at all. It was almost as if he thought the payments were optional, even though he knew the state system was keeping track. Jess wanted to keep the peace with him, so she would nicely remind him to pay his support each month, and he would politely reply that the check was in the mail, but then weeks would go by, and there would still be nothing. If it weren't for the state accounting system, she would have lost track of how far behind he had become.

After witnessing this for months, I advised Jess she would have to put her foot down on this issue or else it would continue like this for years. It cost her almost nothing to file a complaint about enforcement via the state-run system. She may have even done it without a lawyer—just a few clicks on the system's website.

The Pennsylvania court immediately issued a summons for Bill. Apparently, it was lost in the mail, and the summons turned into a bench warrant. I don't know what his defense was when he eventually got to the courtroom because I wasn't there, but I do know the result. After looking over his financial statements, they required him to pay a lump sum of about $4,000 immediately to catch up partially. Then, a few months later, another lump sum of a couple thousand was automatically deducted from the tax refund he was supposed to get from the government. Bill has been much more punctual with his payments ever since then.

You may have noticed we opened this section with *three* payment mechanisms but so far have only mentioned two. The third is a more recent invention: a parenting app called Our Family Wizard or one of its competitors. These apps track everything from child support payments to routine text messages between parents, and they are so practical that some jurisdictions are mandating their use.

Since you never really know whether a person will be punctual or not with their payments in advance, we recommend you just ask for and agree to use the state-run system or a parenting app like Our Family Wizard from the beginning. There may be a small processing fee each month, but other than that, there is no downside, even if you are the parent making the payments, because you too should want a clear record of your payments for all to see. If you are using the do-it-yourself method, it may be harder down the road to prove what you've paid.

Attorney Fees

We've already written at length about how fast your legal bills can mount in a child custody battle. But what we have not told you yet (unless you caught the relevant paragraph in my consent order shown in the last chapter) is that in many states, it is customary for one party to be forced to pay all or some of the other party's legal bills when there is a vast difference in incomes. This blew my mind at the time. The rationale is that the courts don't want the legal system to serve only "the rich."

When the two parties are approximately equal financially, like Jess and Bill were at the time of their custody battle, neither party is likely to owe the other reimbursement for legal fees. Jess paid about $30,000 in legal fees for her relatively simple struggle. There was no chance of reimbursement from Bill or vice versa, even though she would say Bill's initial request for sole custody basically amounted to a frivolous lawsuit. But in my case with Mary, since my income was much higher than hers, Mrs. Big told me I should expect the judge to force me to pay at least some of Mary's legal fees.

This was outrageous to me because if Mary weren't contesting my parenting rights, then there would be almost no legal fees to begin with. I thought merit must play a role in deciding who gets reimbursed and who doesn't. In my view, I was not asking for anything extraordinary. I wanted to pay the standard child support, and I wanted joint legal custody with regular overnight visitation rights. I was told my requests were reasonable and would likely win in court. So why should I have to fund Mary's unreasonable legal battle against me?

Well, because "that's just how it works in Maryland" when one party has a much higher income, I was told. To emphasize the point, my legal complaint actually asked the courts to force Mary to reimburse *my* legal fees, but Mrs. Big told me there was a slim chance of that ever happening since Mary was claiming zero income and I had a big Wall Street paycheck. She said the most I could hope for was to escape paying any of her fees. Perhaps the court would see that her father had been loaning (gifting?) her the money to pay her attorney and therefore rule that she was not at a financial disadvantage.

But once again, compromise is the way you avoid a trial. In my consent order shown in the last chapter, you see that I agreed to pay $10,000 toward Mary's legal fees as part of our settlement. That was just a round number that served as a compromise. She surely paid more than $10,000 to her lawyers, but she didn't want to risk the chance of getting *nothing* from me in a trial. While I thought it was a total injustice to pay *anything* toward her legal bills, I didn't want to risk paying more in a trial. So we compromised on $10,000.

By the end of my year-one custody battle for Kelly, I had paid Mrs. Big $50,000 in fees, and we never even had a trial. Plus, I paid $10,000 to Mary, so $60,000 total in year one. Unfortunately, that wasn't the end of it.

Over the following five years, Mary and I would have four more legal battles due to what I viewed to be her noncompliance with our consent order. Each time the violations were blatant, and I requested in my complaints that the courts make her reimburse my legal expenses due to the merits of my arguments. Still, Mrs. Big always told me to assume it would more likely be the other way around, given our wide income gaps.

Although none of them ended in trials, I ended up paying a portion of Mary's legal expenses as part of our settlements in three of the five battles. Looking back over the entire five-year period, I spent a total of $165,000 in various legal-related fees, of which $21,000 went straight to Mary's attorney fees. It could have been much more if we had ever gone to trial.

Again, the courts don't want to favor the rich, but in my opinion, the rules were too tilted in Mary's favor. Once she understood I could not enforce our agreements without paying some of her legal fees, I believe it emboldened her to abuse her position as the custodial parent. That's my point of view, anyway, and I'm sure Mary's is different. But, as I said before, possession is nine-tenths of the law. She had possession of our child and could, therefore, break our parenting plan regularly with little concern of consequences because even if I dragged her to court, she knew there would be a long delay and she would get at least some of her legal fees paid for.

For example, she would regularly show up late to transitions or refuse to allow my parents to help with transitions, even after one of our legal battles addressed these very questions. She often didn't allowed me to choose my summer vacation days and rarely expanded the days from fourteen, as our original agreement stated. She—well, it doesn't matter what else she did that I felt was not in following with our arrangements. The point is, she knew she could push the envelope because she had almost nothing to lose.

It was only by the fifth battle that she finally agreed to use a parenting coordinator, which largely took her advantage away in this regard. The PC could hear our complaints and make quick decisions without expensive legal battles.

Like everything else, the PC fees were not split 50/50. I paid 90% of those hourly bills, which over almost two years added up to about $9,000 (not included in the $165,000 above). However, unlike attorney fees, the parenting coordinator was worth every penny for reasons discussed in the previous chapter. At least with a parenting coordinator, you get real results.

So for one last time, let us emphasize how important it is to understand that your legal expenses can absolutely crush you. You do need a lawyer, but you don't need to fight every battle in a trial, you don't need to respond legally to everything thrown at you, and you don't need to pay anything close to the bills we paid if you and your co-parent understand there are better ways to get through this. And remember, although this is one of those things that vary from state to state, one party may have to pay a portion of the other party's attorney fees, regardless of the merits of the case.

Recalculating Child Support When Circumstances Change

The last thing to know about child support is that whatever number the court arrives at this year does not have to be the number you use for the next eighteen or twenty-one years (depending on your state). In most states, all you need to recalculate child support is to show there has been a change in circumstances for either party, and it's usually a low bar to qualify for recalculation.

As previously mentioned, there are many legitimate reasons that one or both of your incomes might change. Perhaps you own a start-up business that is struggling at first but later enjoys big success. Or maybe you're a salesperson who rode the wave up selling a hot product, but now your widget is no longer popular, causing your income to crater. Or maybe you are just doing well climbing the corporate ladder, and you earn a pay raise every few years. If either party has a significant and sustained change in income (up or down), then it's probably worth recalculating.

Expenses can also qualify as a change of circumstance, although we believe this can be a little more of a gray area. For example, suppose Jess and I got divorced, and I suddenly owed her alimony and child support for our son on top of splitting half our marital assets. I believe that alone would be a reason to ask the Maryland court to recalculate the child support payment I pay to Mary. Another example of a change in expenses might be if Kelly developed an expensive medical need or if Mary had returned to work sooner and needed to pay for preschool or a nanny.

However, we do not believe that if Mary decided to buy a luxury car or send Kelly to an expensive private school, those sorts of things would qualify as worthy of recalculating support. A change in circumstances does not mean one party *unilaterally* decides to start recklessly spending, thinking the more they spend, the more they will get. However, if Mary and I together *agreed* to send Kelly to an expensive private school, that might be a different story, one in which I may be required to pay more in support.

Furthermore, one party cannot purposely impoverish themselves for the sake of lowering their support bills. If you quit a high-paying job and exchange it for a much lower-paying job, the opposing lawyer will accuse you of self-impoverishment, and the court may very well award a child support number based on your former higher earnings. It might sound crazy, but there are some people who would opt to make less and pay less out of pure spite.

Now, what if you get fired or laid off or downsized? The big question is whether you can find a job with comparable income or not, and sometimes it's not so easy. Our understanding is that in most states, the court will want to see a history of twelve to thirty-six months of earnings when they make a support calculation. If you lose your job this month, you will probably need to wait until you can show at least six to twelve months of lower earnings before you can get a downward revision in support.

It can be frightening to know your child support bill is like a mortgage or rent payment. You are locked in for at least a while, so you had better save up some emergency money in case you find yourself suddenly without income. If you get laid off, you will need to bridge yourself until you can get a revision, and the court will likely want to see you at least try to find comparable employment for a few months before they agree to lower the required payment.

Mary and I have recalculated once in the past ten years, in part because the law in Maryland changed and she wanted to get the new higher number. But the other reason was that I had filed a complaint alleging she was not abiding by our parenting plan, and she countersued for revised child support. Over the years, I learned that just about anytime you go back to court with your co-parent for any reason, there is likely to be a recalculation of child support, so keep that in mind as you weigh the pros and cons of litigation (hint—litigation is seldom worth the trouble). I knew a recalculation in Mary's favor would happen, but things were so bad at the time I felt I had to go through with it, even if it meant paying a lot more in support.

Jess and Bill have never had their child support formally recalculated, even though Bill's income has risen and Jess's has fallen over the years after she stopped working when our son was born. This brings up an important point. Even though

Jess is now married to me, if Jess and Bill were to recalculate their support number, the Pennsylvania court would not count my income in the equation at all. We believe this is fairly standard nationwide; stepparents are not required to financially contribute to stepchildren.

Jess is so turned off by the thought of another court battle that the potentially larger payment is not worth the stress to her. Actually, once this year, Jess agreed to temporarily reverse the child support payment such that she was paying Bill because Adam was staying with him for an entire month during the summer. We figured fair is fair. If we were not feeding Adam this month, we ought to pay the support rather than receiving it. This is unusually generous, but Jess and Bill have developed a great relationship and mutual respect that breeds this sort of cooperation.

While one or two recalculations every ten years is probably average, we have heard stories of people who do it much more frequently. One of our in-laws told us she brought her sons' father back to court every single year, repeatedly getting more money out of him each time. Needless to say, this is not a great way to build a good working relationship with your co-parent. Each trip back to court involves an invasive discovery process (described in chapter 6) along with more attorney fees and months of stressful, sleepless nights. Mrs. Big warned me that some people will ask the court to recalculate every time they see their co-parent with a new car in the driveway.

If your circumstances legitimately change for the medium to long term, then the bottom line is you need to get the child support recalculated. We would recommend attempting to have a civil conversation with your co-parent about the situation before lawyering up. You may be surprised at how reasonable the other party might be, especially if you show them a path that avoids litigation. Ideally, you can then tell your lawyers you already agreed to a new number or a new range and you'd like them to formalize it without going through all the expensive and painful litigation.

Baby Gear—Buy It or Save Your Money?

To close this chapter, we will touch on a lighter financial topic, baby gear. There is an endless supply of baby gear out there. Marketers know darn well who the number-one best customer in the world is: YOU! Especially if this is your first child, you are likely to be a customer who is excited, motivated, and even fearful of not buying enough for your baby.

On top of that, the marketers know first-time parents are often poorly informed, making you an easy target. Here is a quick list of some items you will definitely need to buy, listed in order of "when" you need to buy them.

To buy *before* the birth:

- **A bassinet** — A hand-me-down is fine since you will use this only for a few months. A bassinet is like a mini crib for newborns that fits neatly near the mother's bed. Mom will be picking up the baby every couple of hours for the first few months; and you don't want to let him sleep in your bed with you for safety reasons, so a bassinet is a good investment. Jess had a clever one made with a hinge, so it resembled a tray table you might find in a hospital room. She could easily adjust its position, swinging it closer when she needed to pick up the baby and pushing it farther when she needed to get out of bed, a useful feature when you are still recovering from a C-section and every move you make is difficult.
- **A car seat** — You need to spend the money on a new one because secondhand car seats are not safe and tech-

nically illegal in most places. Make sure it is designed for newborns, and make sure you have it installed and ready to go before your baby arrives. Proper installation in the car is vital, so be sure to read the instructions carefully or get an installation lesson from someone in your community who can help.

- **A changing table and diaper gear** — While a newborn doesn't require his own room, you will want a place where you can safely change a diaper while you are standing, and you will need a supply of newborn-sized diapers. Make sure to get a tube of Vaseline or Aquaphor, which you will need for diaper rashes. You'll need a supply of baby wipes, and unless you like the smell of poopy diapers, invest in a good diaper pail.

- **Infant bathing basin** — These are cheap, but any new parent will tell you how difficult it is to hold an infant with one hand and bathe him with the other. These bathing basins are designed to safely hold the infant in the tub, leaving you two hands free to clean him. Take a look at them online, and you will see what we mean.

- **Thermometer, infant Tylenol, safety nail clippers, and pacifier** — Hopefully, you won't need these on day one. Still, you will need them sooner or later, and the thermometer is especially important to have when you need it. If you call your pediatrician because the baby is not feeling well, one of the first things they will ask is whether she has a fever. Next, they will probably tell you to give her some infant Tylenol. Nails need to be clipped eventually, or else the baby will scratch herself in the face. The hospital will probably send you home with an infant pacifier; it's up to you to decide whether you want to continue using one long-term. Some babies love them, and some don't seem to care about them. We would recommend you try to make do without one at first because there can be some adverse side effects as the child grows teeth, and it can be hard to ween them off it down the road. However, if you find your baby loves his "binky," as my mother called it, don't be afraid to use it. Millions of kids use a pacifier to soothe themselves for a couple of years, with no adverse consequences.

To buy *after* the birth:

- **Nursing gear and breast pump** — The hospital will likely give you some starter nursing gear and instructions to help you start breastfeeding. Take it seriously and give it a legitimate try for a few weeks, at least. Nursing can be challenging but worth the effort. Once you get home and start to figure out what works for you, you will probably want to purchase a breast milk extraction pump and a variety of infant-sized bottles, nipples, nursing bras, etc. But you can wait to see what works for you before you stock up. Concerning breast pumps, Jess feels the cheap and simple suction pumps work perhaps better than the expensive electronic pumps, and the real trick she believes is to pump from one breast while the baby is nursing on the other. Also, be aware health insurance will usually cover the cost of a breast pump but probably only after the child is born, so make sure to look into that before you pay for one out of pocket.

- **Nursery crib and other furniture** — Some mothers go crazy setting up a nursery months before the baby arrives. They buy all the furniture, paint the walls, gather up stuffed animals, the whole nine yards. Then the baby arrives, and it's three months before the baby even uses the room. We understand it's exciting to get set up, but just realize your baby's nursery is not really needed on day one. You can wait to see what you need and want after you get home from the hospital.

A side note about cribs. Mary and I got into a huge argument during the pregnancy when she told me she wanted an expensive crib, and I replied, "We need to buy two cribs, one for your house and one for mine." Recall that she didn't want our baby sleeping at my house for many years, so my comment sparked a terrible argument. She ended up with the crib she wanted, but I don't think Kelly ever slept in it because Mary later became devoted to attachment parenting and co-sleeping in the same bed. I delayed and never bought a crib for my place because I didn't end up with an overnight visit for well over a year, and by then, I realized I would use a hand-me-down crib. Mary and I should not have worried about the crib during the pregnancy, and you shouldn't worry about one, either, especially if you are the visiting parent.

■ **Stroller** — Strollers can be quite expensive, especially if you want a high-performance one designed for jogging or twins. At first, you'll need something that can accommodate an infant; some strollers are designed to transform from an infant stroller to a toddler stroller with extra attachments (sold separately, of course). Jess had an infant stroller intended to easily "unclip" from the stroller wheelbase and "clip-in" to the car seat mount, which helps move the sleeping baby from the stroller to the car. But these fancy designs are usually big, bulky, and expensive. Sometimes, especially as the child gets older, you will just want one of those lightweight, compact "umbrella" strollers, as they are called. You don't need a stroller on day one. Give some thought to what you want and consider saving some money with secondhand equipment from friends or family. You'd be surprised how willing people are to gift you their expensive baby gear that they have no use for anymore.

- **High chair for feeding** — Again, there is a wide selection of high chairs available for you to choose from out there. The good news is you don't need one for a while because your newborn will be lying on his back feeding on a nipple for months. So do some research and look for a hand-me-down if you want to save some money. No rush here.

- **Infant clothes and toys** — If there is one thing you will probably have too much of, it's baby clothes and toys. People will buy you baby gifts, and even if they don't, kids grow out of their clothes, and the toys lose their novelty quickly. Of course, your child will need clothes and some toys, but there is no need to stock up on them before the birth.

- **Baby carrier** — These come in handy after a couple of months home from the hospital when your baby is not quite as fragile as he was at first. There are dozens of brands, sizes, and shapes to choose from; you'll want something that fits your body and the baby's size and age. You may need to experiment a bit, but once you find something that works, it's a great productivity booster to have your infant strapped to your chest with your arms free, and the baby will probably like going along for a ride too. Just make sure whatever you use is safe and the little guy's breathing is not restricted while you are carrying him around.

- **Sleeping gear like Baby Merlin's Magic Sleepsuit** — At first, your newborn will sleep swaddled up in a baby cloth (you will learn all about swaddling at the hospital). But as they transition around age three months away from the swaddle, you will want to try one of these Baby Merlin's Magic Sleepsuits or something similar. Both of Jess's kids were sleeping safely, on their backs, through the entire night at age four months in part due to these sleepsuits. There are competing products out there that are probably also good, but our experience is only with Baby Merlin's Magic Sleepsuit, so that's what we will vouch for here.
- **Pack 'n Play** — I had never heard of this before I was a parent. It may sound like some sort of dance move or video game, but a Pack 'n Play is just a portable crib for infants and babies up to about two years old. They fold up neatly and are a lifesaver anytime you are away from home with your little one and need a safe place to put him down. You don't need it on day one, but it's a great item to put on your baby shower registry.
- **Baby monitor or camera** — Sooner rather than later, you will want to leave the room when the baby is sleeping, and we guarantee you will want a baby monitor or baby camera. The baby cameras they make now are amazing. They connect to your smartphone and can alert you to sound, motion, even change in temperature. They have night vision and all sorts of other smart features. We recommend you buy one that runs on AC power so you are not always charging the battery, and get one that connects to your smartphone so you can watch from anywhere and be alerted to problems in real-time. It is also nice to look back in the video history and see how your sitter behaves when she thinks

she is alone with your baby. Most of these cameras are designed to fit into a larger home surveillance package of equipment, so you may want to consider the bigger picture before you rush out and buy the first baby camera you find.

- **Sleeping sound machine** — This is one of those things people don't think of unless they sleep with one themselves. Jess and I swear by a noisemaker at night, and we believe it helps our children sleep too. They are cheap, and when you want your child to sleep, every little trick in the book helps.

- **Books** — Speaking of books, you will want some baby books to read to the baby, but you will also want some adult books about babies. The time to read these is now, while you have the little one to practice on in real-time. If you read all this stuff during the pregnancy, you'll forget a lot when the time comes, and if you wait too long to read them, well, then it won't matter much anymore. As mentioned previously, we strongly recommend *Eat, Poop, Sleep* by Dr. Scott Cohen for baby's first year, and as she gets a little older, take a look at *Parenting with Love & Logic* by Foster Cline and Jim Fay. There are countless others, of course.

Save your money and don't bother with these items:

- **Bottle warmers** — There are plenty of ways to warm a bottle without a fancy device.

- **Bottle sterilizers** — If your kitchen has a dishwasher or even just a sink with hot water and soap, there is no need for a separate machine that does the same thing.

- **Baby wipe warmer** — This device warms the sanitary wipes before using them to wipe up the baby's poop. Don't waste your money. The baby will never miss it.

- **Infant walkers** — This is one of those little baby chairs mounted on wheels, allowing the baby to move himself around without holding up his own weight. Pediatricians now say these can impede the natural learning-to-walk process, so best to stay away from these old-fashioned walkers.
- **Snot suckers** — This is basically just a tube you stick up baby's nose and then literally suck the snot out by sucking with your mouth on the other end of the tube. Babies had cleared their mucus for millions of years before someone bought the first infant snot sucker. We think this is a prime example of marketers instilling fear in new parents. On the other hand, my sister-in-law thinks these things are indispensable, so we don't know. Maybe pick one up; after all, they are only a couple bucks.

8 | Getting Along for the Long Term

I f you have read this far, you have done yourself a great service. You got many of your basic questions answered without paying by the hour for the information. You now know how to be laser-focused when meeting with your attorney on the questions only they can answer for you.

You learned about pregnancy issues, what legal and physical custody is all about, and how to think about child support and other financial matters. You know enough right now to get you through your child's first year without having a nervous breakdown and, hopefully, without breaking the bank.

This last chapter will answer some of those lingering questions you may still have while at the same time offering a bit of practical advice on how to get along with your co-parent for the long term. These are the sorts of things you may not give much thought to now but are sure to matter in the longer run.

What If I Want to Move?

The chances are good that either you or your co-parent will want to relocate at some point in the next eighteen years. People move for marriage, for jobs, and for all kinds of other reasons. During her pregnancy, Mary expressed to me that she intended to move from the East Coast to the West Coast after our child was born. She never did, but the possibility led me to research the subject, as did Jessica's experience relocating inside Pennsylvania.

Jessica and Bill had hammered out their custody arrangement in the Philadelphia court system because that's where they both lived at the time. Like many other parenting agreements, it stated the co-parents would share the travel burden equally for visits. As previously mentioned, she had primary physical custody of Adam, and Bill had visitation rights every other weekend.

A couple of years after signing their agreement, Jessica decided to move about three hours away to Harrisburg, Pennsylvania. Pennsylvania law holds a "relocation hearing" if one parent is protesting the other parent's move. In that hearing, the judge told Jess she was free to move wherever she liked, but she would have to bear the additional travel burden that her move caused her co-parent, Bill. In other words, if she wanted to move to Harrisburg, she would have to drive her son back to Philly every other weekend to visit his father. So that's what she did.

A few years later, Jessica moved back to the Philadelphia area, and around the same time, Bill moved out to Ohio for a job. Since he opted to move far away, he is now the one who does the long-distance traveling to see his son every few weeks.

While this was going on in Pennsylvania between Jessica and Bill, I learned the rules concerning relocations were slightly different in Maryland. Or maybe the rules were the same but applied differently to me because I was already located four hours away in New York, whereas Jess and Bill started nearby each other. Mrs. Big explained that, unlike Jessica's situation in Pennsylvania, if Mary wanted to move across the state, it would *not* automatically mean she had to make up the extra travel time. Indeed, Mrs. Big drove it home to me that this was America, and the courts could not stop anyone from moving anywhere they wanted, including out of state.

All Mrs. Big could say for sure was that no matter where Mary and Kelly ended up, I would have a right to see my child but I may have to fight a new battle in that new locality if Mary didn't cooperate. Perhaps, she said, if the distance were far enough, I would have to accept different visitation terms. For example, if Mary moved to California and I stayed in New York, I probably would not want to be flying the child across the country every other weekend for years to come. In that case, the courts would make some other arrangements, such as long weekends once a month with more extended visits in the summer.

Again, Jess was told a different story by her lawyers in Pennsylvania. She was told if she moved far away, she would have to bear the extra travel burden or perhaps even give up physical custody. We believe this is one of those issues that vary from state to state and situation to situation, so be sure to consult with your attorney on this topic.

Mary and I addressed the potential problem by agreeing in our parenting plan that "Each party shall afford the other 90 days written notice via email of any intended change of address of more than 25 miles from any major Amtrak station, including or between Union Station in Washington, DC, and Penn Station in New York City, NY." I remember the attorneys saying a ninety-day written notice was required in Maryland in advance of any relocation, regardless of what we wrote in our agreement. We assume there are similar rules in other states.

We are not trying to worry you about all the what-ifs. The point is that people move all the time, and your parenting situation will have to adapt one way or another. Just be prepared to make some sacrifices if you are the party who initiates the move. And make sure to consider how the move will affect your child. Do you really want them to spend hours in the car or train or airplane every other weekend for years to come? We can tell you from experience that long-distance traveling is stressful for kids, especially as they get older and sports and social calendars start to interfere with your out-of-town visitation plans. If you want to get along for the long term, try to live as close as possible to your co-parent.

Makeup Visits

Sports and birthday parties may not be much of an issue right now while your child is young, but from day one, there will be many reasons you want to alter the regular schedule as defined in your parenting plan. Some events like a family wedding are known well in advance, while others like a blizzard or sudden illness are last minute in nature.

When these inevitable situations arise, how will you and your co-parent handle them? Will you go strictly by the book, or will you make exceptions for each other? Mary and I didn't address makeup visits in our parenting plan, but we took the approach that we needed to be flexible to help each other. Mary hated driving in snow, so when there was terrible weather, I did all the driving or moved the weekend to another weekend. For significant family events like weddings, we requested a schedule change far in advance.

To Mary's credit, she always allowed me to make up my time with Kelly, even though makeup visits were not addressed in our agreement. It's just the right thing to do, and besides, there were plenty of weekends when she needed me to reciprocate the favor. My only complaint with Mary in this regard was that she often procrastinated in committing to a makeup weekend for my visit. She would say something like, "I'll look at the calendar and let you know what works," and then weeks would go by before she would commit to a makeup date.

This drove me crazy, and it wasn't until we started meeting with our parenting coordinator that she learned how important it was to commit to makeup dates in a timely manner. It should go without saying, if you are the party asking for a change to the regular schedule, then at the very same time you ask for the change, make sure to offer up a few choices for makeup visits and allow the other parent to pick the one that works best for them. Fair is fair.

As your child gets older, there will be many visits that need to be moved due to games, parties, recitals, family events, funerals, weather, illness, etc., and your idea of what constitutes a switch may not be the same as your co-parent's. A parenting coordinator can help you work out which events are worthy of changing the schedule and which are just not important enough. Be flexible and fair, and you will get along for the long term.

Transitioning the Child from Parent to Parent

If you live near your co-parent, transitioning your child from one home to another should not be too much of an issue, but here are a few tips. First, find a routine that is your default routine so you don't need to discuss it each visit. Maybe Dad picks the child up Friday night from Mom's house, and Mom picks up from Dad's place on Sundays. We recommend having the parent who is receiving the child do the picking up because this will encourage punctuality.

Punctuality can be a big issue. Mary and I had a long-distance trip to deal with, and we constantly battled over when and where to meet and how to control excessive lateness. I often used the Amtrak trains between New York and Washington, DC, so I was uptight about being punctual so as not to miss my train. Mary preferred to drive and refused to allow extra time for traffic, so she would frequently arrive late when she dropped off Kelly, saying, "Sorry, traffic again."

If you have a long distance to travel and can incorporate a train into your routine, I highly recommend it. Kids love riding on trains, and it can be an excellent time to bond. Of course, trains can run late, but they are usually more reliable than highway traffic and much safer statistically than spending hours in the car each week.

Anyway, punctuality is a type A/type B personality issue that can cause problems if you refuse to at least attempt to understand the other person's point of view. Mary is one of those people who is late for everything, while I try to be early all the time. She never thought much of it if she was twenty, forty, or even sixty minutes late. On the other hand, I viewed her tardiness as a purposeful theft of my already short visitation time. We both handled it poorly, but lateness sure caused many arguments between us over the years.

You should also allow other family members or childcare providers to participate in transitions sometimes. Nannies, grandparents, even stepparents may need to fill in for you or your co-parent at a pickup or drop-off, and hopefully, you won't find any reason to protest their help. Mary's mother frequently did her leg of the traveling for her. However, Mary always refused to drop off Kelly with my parents. She would say the visits were for me only and would hold Kelly back until I could be physically present for the drop-off. Of course, I saw it differently, and this issue was another cause of frequent arguments that I'll never fully understand.

I tried all sorts of tricks to solve our transition problems. To address the lateness, someone advised we meet at a fast-food restaurant and buy something to document the time with the cash register receipt. The timestamp on the receipt is supposedly proof you are on time, although it doesn't really prove the other parent is late unless she also gets a receipt. I thought about bringing Kelly home late on Sundays when she arrived late Fridays, but that didn't work, either because I had a train to catch or because Mary would just use my Sunday lateness as an excuse to be even later the following Friday. Attorneys told us some parents who cannot be civil with each other meet at police stations, but thankfully, Mary and I were never that bad.

One of our subsequent legal battles addressed these transition issues in my favor, and yet Mary still refused to drop off Kelly with anyone but me, and she has never gotten much better about being on time. Eventually, I realized there is just not much that can be done about someone who refuses to be punctual unless you get a parenting coordinator involved. Regardless of your situation, try to remember that getting along for the long term means you must be respectful of each other's time, be flexible in transition arrangements, and at the very least, make sure to call if you are going to be late.

Religion

For some people these days, religion just isn't much of an issue, especially if both parents belong to the same faith (not much to argue about in that case). If the parents are of different religions and don't feel strongly about it, then it's probably fine to have your child attend church with Mom and syna-gogue with Dad or whatever the case may be. But sometimes, one parent does feel strongly about religion, as was the case with Mary.

Mary and I had some discussions about religion during our first custody battle. She was concerned I might try to interfere with Kelly's religion and she would miss too many Sunday services when she was with me. I was worried I might be forced to spend my limited time in hours of religious ser-vices with a church I did not belong to. Mrs. Big informed me that if we left it to the judge to decide, he would typically assign religion to the parent with primary physical custody, so in our case, Mary. However, she said the courts would not force me to take Kelly to services on my time.

We solved both our concerns by writing in the parenting plan that Kelly would be raised with Mary's religion but nei-ther Mary nor I would be required to attend church services with Kelly on Sunday. This is reasonable and works for most people. After all, everyone misses services now and then, no matter how devout you are, so Mary could not require me to attend services if she wasn't required to attend herself. If you want to get along for the long term, you cannot argue about religion year after year, and the parent with physical custody will eventually win the battle.

Stepparents

For infants and toddlers, you shouldn't have a big problem with stepparents. Babies love anyone with whom they spend a lot of time, assuming they are shown kindness. It's only as your child grows older and starts to wonder why Mom is not married to Dad that problems can arise.

This is the pattern we saw with Kelly and Adam growing up, for sure. Adam treated me like a second father, and Kelly loved spending time with Jessica for the first five or so years we were all together. But ever since about age nine, things have started to change. The kids have started to resent the fact their birth parents are not together, and it shows clearly in various conscious and subconscious behaviors that can be upsetting and frustrating.

But teenager challenges are beyond the scope of this book. For now, you need to prepare yourself for the probable scenario that your child will likely have one or two stepparents in his life. This can be difficult for some parents to stomach, especially if you are the visiting parent, because it might mean the stepparent spends more time with your child than you do.

Try your best to respect boundaries and always worry first about your child's feelings more than your own. If your child likes their stepparent, try to be supportive. If they don't like them for some reason, then find out why but recognize many kids develop a natural aversion to stepparents as they grow older. Talk to your child about it and talk to your co-parent about it to make sure there are no serious issues. Try to identify the problem while at the same time trusting that your co-parent also wants what's best for the child.

Stepparenting can be a tricky, complicated thing that probably won't get any easier in the teenage years. The last thing you want to do is badmouth your co-parent's new spouse. This sort of thing serves no purpose but to twist up your child's head with conflicting thoughts. Remember, it's a lot harder on the child than it is on you, so try to be a good role model with both your words and actions. Kids will always gravitate to healthy parenting, so strive for that and avoid stepparenting drama as much as you can. Of course, if you sense any signs of abuse, then you have to speak up until your concerns are addressed. But otherwise, for the most part, you will have to let your co-parent handle their household dynamics if you want to get along for the long term.

Discipline—Different Homes, Different Rules

Discipline and house rules are another area that can cause problems between co-parents. Since every household is different, your child will likely have some different rules in each home. The parent with physical custody often complains that the visiting parent has lax rules and every visit is just a holiday weekend that spoils the child rotten.

This stereotype probably has some truth to it, because the visiting parent typically doesn't want to spend their short time enforcing rules or chores or discipline. They want the child to look forward to their time visiting, and it can seem silly to worry about things like bedtimes or screen time when you have only a few nights a month together. I'm guilty of this behavior, for sure. When Kelly is with me and doesn't want to try a food Jessica cooked for dinner, I sometimes let her get away with making something else she likes to eat. But when Adam says he doesn't like it, we say, "Sorry. One family, one meal."

I rationalize this double standard by telling myself Adam lives with us full-time but what's the point of forcing Kelly when I have her only a few days a month? I figure I can't change her behavior if I don't see her every day. This is probably wrong. Kids respect routine and rules for the most part, even if they don't admit it. We recommend you try to treat your visiting child with the same rules as you would if they lived with you full-time.

On the other hand, if you are the parent who is frustrated by different rules in the other home, then you can always try to have a conversation about it with your co-parent. However, whether your parenting agreement specifies it or not, we believe you should follow the language written in my consent order: "It is agreed that the parent with whom the child is at any time residing will have day-to-day parental responsibility of the child and each will respect the other's judgment. Each parent recognizes the other has the child's best interests at heart."

In short, you have to remember there are "different houses, different rules." With Mom, bedtime is nine o'clock, but Dad allows ten o'clock. With Dad, shoes must come off in the house. With Mom, you have to finish your plate if you want dessert. You get the idea. "Different houses, different rules" is a good response when older children try to push back against one parent's rules, and it's also a good response when one co-parent is not respecting the other's right to make day-to-day decisions. Of course, infants don't argue much about rules, but for them, it's probably best to try to follow the routines they are used to at the primary custodian's home for bedtimes, meals, and so on.

Communication

If you have a good working relationship with your co-parent, it's probably because you communicate well. If you don't, the opposite is likely true. Mary and I had dysfunctional communication beginning with the pregnancy that has only recently improved. We use to get into long-winded email and text arguments, often over nothing important or due to written word misunderstandings. When we tried to talk on the phone or in person, it would just lead to yelling. Once our first legal battle began, we realized every communication would be submitted as evidence, and we pretty much stopped communicating altogether. You don't want to end up like Mary and I were back then.

It wasn't until we met with the parenting coordinator that Mary and I relearned how to communicate, but even then, it was far from what I would call quality communication. Nowadays, we have an occasional phone call to discuss schedules or problems, but she still doesn't like to put much in writing, which I find very problematic. When trying to keep track of complicated dates and schedules, it is important to have the details in writing to avoid misunderstandings. Furthermore, for high-conflict parents who seem to argue every time they speak, sticking to written communication can help keep tensions down.

Our parenting coordinator stressed the value of keeping communication "business-like" using email, text, and a shared online calendar, like a Google Calendar. A shared calendar is an excellent way to put the child's schedule all in one place. You put in recurring events like "Weekend Visit with Dad" or "July 4th with Mom in Odd Years" so you can look out years in the future and know who has the child on a given date. You can even mark down transition details like "meeting at train station at 5 pm Friday." When they get older, it's a huge help to see your child's extracurricular activities laid out in one place. It's great because you don't need to have a long discussion about simple dates; you can just check the calendar.

Jessica and I have recently discovered co-parenting apps that take the shared calendar idea one step further. The most popular one out there is called Our Family Wizard, mentioned in an earlier chapter. Apps like this cover the basic calendar and communication functions well, but they also seamlessly share school report cards, photos, expense receipts, requests for payment, medical information, etc. Some parents use it for paying/receiving child support payments, which is great for tracking. There are many other useful built-in functions. For example, if one parent needs to switch weekends, a feature lets them request the schedule change and then documents the other parent's response. While most of these tasks can be completed with a simple email, the apps keep everything in one place, avoiding confusion and miscommunication. For co-parents stuck in dysfunctional or high-conflict relationships, the app can mean all the difference in the world.

Our Family Wizard is such an effective tool that many jurisdictions around the country mandate parents use it for all communication and co-parenting functions. The data that the app tracks, including text messages, calendar appointments, child support payments, and expense reimbursements, are all admissible as evidence and impossible to tamper with by either party. A friend of ours going through a high-conflict divorce recently told us her ex was harassing her with endless messages via the Our Family Wizard. The court reprimanded him after seeing the evidence in the report the app produced. What a fantastic tool! The saying "A little sunlight is the best disinfectant" applies here.

My experience would have been totally different if Mary and I had used Our Family Wizard. Mary was never even willing to *try* an online calendar, which baffles me to this day. I think she liked to keep a paper calendar instead and just didn't like using technology. Our parenting coordinator insisted we emailed each other with important dates and times, and we recommend you at least do that if you are not willing to use a shared online calendar or a co-parenting app.

Unfortunately, once we stopped working with the PC, Mary stopped emailing me as well. Now everything between us is done via voice call or text message. While it is healthy to have a conversation now and then, you still want a written record for dates and schedules. It's frustrating to me that Mary won't email, but it's one of those things I have learned to just accept regarding our different personality types.

You may recall the story from an earlier chapter about the judge who told Mary and me about the co-parents who didn't communicate well. Their teenage daughter snuck out of the house, telling each parent she was with the other. She ended up dead that night. If the parents had just communicated better, their child would still be alive. Don't let this sort of thing happen to you.

No matter how much you hate talking to your co-parent, you have to find a way to communicate the basics, at least. Keep the conversations and messages fact-based: who, what, where, when. No sarcasm. No teasing. No hostile comments. Don't send long-winded written messages about your feelings or concerns when a phone call would be better. Remember, written words tend to lose the tone, and everything you write to each other will be considered evidence if you end up back in court someday. Follow the newspaper rule: if you wouldn't want your message printed on the front page of the newspaper, then don't write it in an email or text.

Lastly, never ask your child to carry a message to your co-parent. They don't want to be the messenger between their parents. It makes them feel uncomfortable and as if they have to choose sides. The words "Tell your mom I want to switch weekends" or "Tell your dad I want to drop you off late next visit" should never come out of your mouth. Always go directly to your co-parent for communications.

You are going to have disagreements over the years with your co-parent. Every parent does, whether you are married or not. The key is to learn how to talk it out like responsible adults or, at the least, learn how to communicate the basics with a parenting app.

Child Comes First

This may sound obvious, but every decision you make for the rest of your life should consider the question, *How will this affect my child?* We are not saying your life has to revolve around them. But you need to pause at least and consider your child all the time.

Are you thinking of moving out of state or even out of town? How will that affect your child's visitation schedule?

Want your new boyfriend/girlfriend to move in with you? How will that affect your child if you break up with this person in six months?

Are you considering writing a book about co-parenting? What will your daughter think of it if she discovers the book as a teenager?

Big decisions like those three above should prompt you to consider your child. But it's the smaller, day-to-day things that can sometimes fall through the cracks. Do not bad-mouth your co-parent or their family in front of your child, no matter how old they are. You'd be shocked at how much kids understand before they can even speak. Bad-mouthing your co-parent just makes your child uncomfortable and resentful, and eventually will only encourage them to lie to you about their time with the parent you are critical of.

Play fair and by the book. If Mom is late every weekend or canceling visits altogether, don't withhold child support payments as revenge or ransom. For one thing, the courts will not agree with your strategy; they will just say, "Two wrongs don't make a right." But more important, your child will probably suffer if they don't have the benefit of your child support payment. If your co-parent is not following your parenting agreement, then talk to a lawyer or try to get a parenting coordinator involved, but never ever withhold child support payments.

The opposite is also true. If your co-parent is not paying their support, do not try to withhold visitation. Again, the courts will not look kindly on that behavior, and more important, how will your child feel if they don't get to see their other parent this weekend?

The child comes first. Always. It doesn't mean you should spoil them or that nothing else matters. It just means consider them in every decision you make, and you will get along much better with your co-parent in the long term.

The Big Picture

Try to see the big picture. You and your co-parent are not in love, and you may not even get along, but you are bound for the rest of your lives by the love and concern you have for your child's well-being. When you find yourself arguing, take a deep breath and try to remember you are both on the same team, fighting for the same end goal. You just see the path differently right now, but you are headed in the same direction.

Try to remember you will need your co-parent's help dozens and dozens of times over the years. Favors like switching the schedule or accommodating other requests go a long way toward building a good working relationship. If you find yourself automatically saying no when you could be saying yes, then you are probably reacting out of anger or spite more than anything else. If it helps, think of every favor you do as an IOU that you will get back someday when the time comes that you need something.

And you need your co-parent for more than just favors. You need them to take good care of your child when you are not around, and your child needs both parents to play a role. It's hard enough for a child to grow up with separated parents, so do what you can to make it easier for your co-parent to be at their best when they are on duty. Make sure your child has their favorite toys or other items available to bring on visits and make sure to send her home with those items. Encourage a few pictures of the other parent in your child's bedroom in your home. Don't just avoid bad-mouthing your co-parent; go out of your way to talk them up in front of your child.

Respect the day-to-day decision-making of the parent with the child. It's fine to discuss significant issues, but no one wants to be micromanaged by a co-parent. Offer your advice but realize there is more than one way to do things, and it won't kill your child to get a different perspective on an issue from his other parent. On the contrary, getting two *different* viewpoints is precisely the benefit of having two parents. Don't deprive your child of his co-parent's perspective, even if you disagree with it.

Finally, at moments of stress, try to sit back and think of the long term, the big picture. Ten years will fly by in a flash. Right now, you are obsessing over short-term problems, but your child will be grown up and moving out of the house before you know it, and all these arguments you had in year one will seem trivial when you look back at them someday. Pick your battles carefully; it is incredible how the smallest comment can spark an inferno of relationship problems. Always try to see the big picture, and we promise, in the long run, you will get along much better with your co-parent—and your child will be better off for it too.

Connect with Us

Jessica and I would love to interact with you. If you find this book helpful, want to learn more, have any criticism of our advice, or just want to share your story, please visit our website, BabyOutOfWedlock.com. We are experimenting with services that might help you in your journey, as well as useful links and blog posts with the most up-to-date information out there, all in one place. And remember, everything you learned here is most effective if your co-parent knows it, too, so make sure to point them in our direction.

Remember the stat we told you in chapter 1: the CDC says nearly 40% of all births in the United States are to unmarried parents. Help us help the millions of other parents like you who need this information. If this book was effective for you, please help us reach more people by leaving a review on Amazon or any other platform, and then pass the word on to your family law attorney, OB-GYN, therapists, or anyone else who might come in contact with parents like you.

You are not alone. You can do this if you keep a positive attitude about it. We wish you a happy, healthy new chapter in your life as a parent and co-parent.